Praise For *Self-Esteem F...*

"This is an invaluable book. Dr. Schweiger write... ... ... seasoned professional and personal experience and expertise. Without judgment, and with a great deal of compassion, she provides parents with a blueprint for nurturing their children's self-esteem, the foundation for all happiness and well-being. An essential book that can benefit all."

— Amy Hatkoff, *You Are My World: How a Parent's Love Shapes a Baby's Mind*

"Dr. Ingrid Schweiger is one of the warmest, brightest and most caring psychologists that I have met. Having published the leading trade magazine in talk media for almost two decades, I have met quite a few, including the stars of the field. Her years of experience and down-to-earth approach to relationships come across in this book clearly and with remarkable effectiveness. The road to a healthy society begins with loving and positive parenting. This book is a most valuable guide in taking us there."

— Michael Harrison, Publisher of *Talkers Magazine*

"Today's parents are inundated by warnings, overwhelmed by choices and overextended by errands and activities. Dr. Schweiger's book culls through life's distractions and brings her readers safely back to the parenting basics of listening and communication. Her practical advice on raising happy children and nurturing family relationships is wise and effective. This book is a 'must-read' for parents, especially those with stressful, busy lives. We're guessing that's you."

— Conner Herman and Kira Ryan, Dream Team Baby and TheBump.com

"*Self-Esteem For A Lifetime* encourages parents and grandparents to help build up our younger generations. Due to the busy-ness of our lives, children often receive the wrong messages. Dr. Schweiger gently shares positive ways to slow down and do what is in the best interest of our youth. Her real life examples, lists, questions, and stories offer useful tactics for intentional, positive communication between the generations which builds the self-esteem and quality of lives in the children we so tenderly love."

— Dotsie Bregel, Founder of the National Assoc. of Baby Boomer Women

Self-Esteem For A Lifetime

Raising A Successful Child From The Inside Out

Enjoy your family!
Ingrid

by

Dr. Ingrid Schweiger

authorHOUSE®

AuthorHouse™
1663 Liberty Drive, Suite 200
Bloomington, IN 47403
www.authorhouse.com
Phone: 1-800-839-8640

First published by AuthorHouse 9/8/2008

ISBN: 978-1-4343-7225-3 (sc)

Printed in the United States of America
Bloomington, Indiana

This book is printed on acid-free paper.

To my loving family

ACKNOWLEDGEMENTS

Many people helped to make this book a reality. Thank you to my daughters Jenn and Rebecca, my son-in-law Rob, Janice Masters and Michael Harrison for your valuable support and encouragement. Words cannot express my appreciation to my husband Joseph for his generous warmth, understanding and love.

Thank you to the many men, women and families I have worked with during the last thirty years. You have enriched my life in many ways. I appreciate your openness, trust and confidence in me.

CONTENTS

INTRODUCTION

Building your child's self esteem is a process that begins at birth and continues throughout a lifetime. In *Self-Esteem for a Lifetime,* you will learn how building your child's self-esteem influences:

- How and what your child achieves
- How your child socializes
- How your child loves
- How your child will make decisions throughout his/her life

I am writing this book for parents, educators and all people who love children to help prevent the development of difficulties for their children, as well as to offer help when a problem does occur. As I examine thirty years of experience with children, their parents, and people in general, I find self-esteem to be the core ingredient for success in every arena of life. It is self-esteem that influences all of our behaviors, choices and decisions. If you were to observe those suffering emotional, behavior and relationship problems, you would find low self-esteem to be the common denominator in all cases.

I wanted to write a book that focuses on the essence of the parent-child relationship, the most significant relationship for any child. My work, research and lectures have addressed many different aspects of raising children and family dynamics. I decided to concentrate on isolating the "key" element in a child who is happy with himself/herself and happy with the world. Once I collected all of my thoughts, self-esteem stood out loud and clear. Believing as I do that parents are the real experts, I gathered with groups of parents in order to hear their ideas, observe their responses and share our stories. This process is what this book is all about. Listening and learning from all the families I have worked with paved the way. I am so grateful and honored to have been welcomed into the private lives of so many. I cherish your trust in me.

This book in many ways represents my own personal and professional odyssey. It feels as though I have lived several lifetimes since my days as an elementary school teacher in Syracuse, New York in 1969. Since that time, I have been a wife, a mother, a single parent, a wife again, a mother-in-law and a grandmother and have met thousands of families in so many different settings. My career has taken me from the office to radio, television, college campuses and lecturing in a wide variety of settings.

Parenting is the most difficult job in the world. Who prepares us? My greatest challenge and most demanding role, without a shadow of a doubt, has been raising my two daughters, now 31 and 35. My own family has definitely been my most significant laboratory for learning. I often revisit the ideas presented in this book in order to refresh my skills and improve my relationships with my two adult children.

Regardless of how hard I work at it, I must often remind myself, "There are no perfect parents!" On the other hand, parents can make a tremendous difference. With all of this responsibility, most of us are faced with anxieties, fears and self-doubt. How many times have you asked yourself that age-old question, "DID I DO THE RIGHT THING?" Read on to gain the confidence, and learn new skills that will help you and your children every step of the way.

I began writing this book with the hopes of offering parents assistance and support with the challenge of raising young children. As I complete this project, though, I can see that all of the concepts and suggestions I make apply to your relationships with your children at any age. In fact, building self-esteem in others will improve all of your relationships and have a profound impact on how you feel about yourself. I hope this book feels like a helping hand, offers food for thought, and becomes a friend to confide in. Raising children today is a unique challenge. With the many changes in society, there are so many new stresses on both parents and children. It is my hope that this book offers you the knowledge, support, and reassurance that all of us need. Self-esteem is a gift your family will treasure today, tomorrow and for many years to come.

Sincerely,

Dr. Ingrid Schweiger

1

WHAT IS SELF-ESTEEM?

What is self-esteem? As I questioned parents both in my groups and individually, I heard a variety of interpretations and stories that spanned the generations:

There was this time in high school when I became the most popular guy, after years of feeling like the ugly duckling. It felt like an overnight transformation. One day, I looked in the mirror and hated everything I was. The next day, it was like it all came together. My grades improved and kids started to talk to me and include me. I felt really proud of myself! I wish I could make that happen for my son...

It seems as though my daughter has been struggling with everything. I don't want to make her feel worse than she already feels. I can't stop looking over her school work each day and helping her every night on the day's assignments. Unfortunately, I become so frustrated. I know I say a lot of things I shouldn't say. It seems like the more I care, the more her grades are dropping. Of course, our entire household revolves around her school work. Her self-esteem? Well, she has none. She behaves like one big failure and I guess, if I were to be honest with myself, I also see her as a failure. How do I help her to like herself again? How do I help myself?

The stories kept coming. Some parents described children with specific difficulties in school, at home or with friends. Some parents felt that although they were not experiencing any specific problems with their children, they wanted to develop the tools to help build their child's self-image and self-confidence. These parents felt that their children needed additional "armor" to tackle the challenges that lie ahead. Although no two parents shared the same situation, the common thread was extremely strong. We all cared deeply about our children. We all felt that this force - "self-esteem" - was vital in order to energize our children and ensure that they would maximize their strengths and be able to live with their limitations.

Self-esteem can be thought of as the sum total of accumulated feelings and evaluations about yourself that add up to your sense of self-worth. Self-esteem answers the question: How much do I value myself?

What does self-esteem mean to you?

_____

_____

_____

_____

How would you recognize a child with high self-esteem? Often, you can feel his energy. A child with high self-esteem believes in himself, and is ready to tackle a challenge. Self-esteem is written all over someone's face and is reflected in the ways a person walks and talks. A child with high self-esteem may make comments like:

- "I like me."

- "I made a new friend today."

- "School is fun."

- "My teacher thinks I'm nice."

- "I enjoy trying something new."

The parents in the group added many other statements they have heard their children use and gestures they have seen when self-esteem was running high.

- "I love reading."

- "I want to start a new project."

- "Mom, can I join the baseball team?"

- Storming home from school with a smile.

Self-esteem is an ongoing process. It is not a fixed characteristic, as in certain physical attributes like blue eyes. Eyes that are blue will be blue next year and ten years from now. Not so with self-esteem. When I think of the many children and families I have worked with, it is low self-esteem that brought most people into my office. Low self-esteem is often the underlying problem in a child with behavior problems, social problems, eating disorders, and drug and alcohol addiction.

What happens when a child enters into treatment with a psychologist, psychiatrist, social worker, school psychologist or guidance counselor? To resolve the problems, a course of action is taken to increase your child's self-esteem. The "helper" is looking for strengths and reinforcing the goodness of each child. This loving relationship offers healing and helps a child to feel strong and offers encouragement to experiment with new behavior.

A young woman who stutters called me on the radio one day when I was discussing self-esteem. She described the negative treatment she received for so many years from fellow students and several teachers. She called in order to talk about the non-stop encouragement her parents gave her. Presently, the young woman is in college and feels that she has been able to overcome many obstacles put before her. You could hear her courage and self-confidence, despite her speech problem. This woman is a wonderful example of high self-esteem and the power of positive reinforcement.

A young man who I have been treating for approximately two years originally came in at age 21 feeling suicidal. As I became better acquainted with him and his father, I saw a child who just felt defeated. He was living at home and was totally isolated socially. Although working, his job presented no challenge. His father made it clear to me that this was all the boy was capable of and suggested I leave well enough alone. During our sessions, the young man described the atrocious treatment he received from his peers growing up and the total absence of praise and encouragement from his parents. Today, this young man has undergone such a complete metamorphosis that he even looks like a new person. We laughed as he described the reactions he received at a recent high school reunion: "Is that you?" Today, this young man is in a new job, a college graduate and quite involved in local politics. He has new friends, new activities and complains that there isn't enough time to do everything he would like to do. When I told him about this book, he described feeling for years that this "energy" - self-esteem - was inside of him, but he just couldn't release it.

What made the difference for this young man? Someone was listening to him, seeing his strengths, encouraging him, offering approval and providing a safety net when things didn't go just right. No magic! Parents can provide all of this and more for their children. At any age, it is never too late to help your child unleash this positive life energy, self-esteem. With the stresses of everyday life we have many moments when our behavior as parents is tested but, fortunately, we are presented constantly with new opportunities to listen, encourage and love. As you and your children learn and grow together, continue to remind yourself that there are no perfect parents.

What statements have you heard when your child's self-esteem is high?

What behaviors have you observed?

_____

_____

_____

_____

Describe your own thoughts and behaviors when your self-esteem is running high.

_____

_____

_____

_____

Low Self-Esteem

Low self-esteem is a different story. A child with low self-esteem does not like himself and feels inferior and inadequate. A child with low self-esteem can be heard making statements like:

- "No one likes me."

- "I'm in the low group."

- "I don't want to go to school."

- "I don't want to play with anyone."

- "I can't do that."

When I discussed low self-esteem with parents, everyone had examples to share of low grades, labels assigned in the classroom, teasing, sibling rivalry and changes in the family that had a negative effect on their children's behavior. A number of parents talked of situations when their children's involvement in sports became an incredibly negative experience. One mother told of her seven-year-old child's experience playing soccer. The coach pushed the children, screamed at the children, and even humiliated them at the games in front of their families and friends. It seemed that her son couldn't do anything right. Even when he did score a goal, the coach completely ignored this as if to say, "It's about time." Her seven-year-old became confused and withdrawn. His self-esteem had really taken a beating. This same mother overheard another parent ask the coach after his child did not perform well at the game, "Should I punish him?"

I can't tell you how many children I have observed in the classroom and in my office who simply look as if they have the weight of the world on their shoulders! They have already been teased, rejected, and experienced failure by a very young age. Children constantly look toward their parents for the approval and acceptance that they need so desperately. As many parents in the group shared, "I don't always stop what I'm doing to give him a hug. I get so caught up in the day-to-day routine. I'm exhausted from work, the phone is ringing, I have to get to an appointment, I have to drive one of the kids somewhere, or I just don't think of it." Many parents felt that their criticism and complaints stood out many times over again compared to their positive messages.

Do you find yourself making many statements like:

- "I can't stand this."

- "Clean up that mess."

- "Do I have to listen to this again?"

- "You'll never amount to anything if you don't work harder."

- "Didn't we show you the right way to behave?"

- "Why can't you make us proud of you?"

- "I wish I never had kids."

As one father commented, when everything is running smoothly in the house, there tends to be very little interaction. "You do your thing, I'll do my thing." But, at the slightest provocation, sparks are flying. His involvement is a consequence of something going wrong. What a message for a child. "If you want me to pay attention, aggravate me." Let's face it. We all get caught in this trap.

Self-Concept

Self-concept and self-esteem go hand in hand and are difficult to view separately. Self-concept is a reflection of the way you perceive your attitudes and behaviors. Self-concept answers the question, "What kind of person am I?"

Children (and adults) with high self-esteem and a positive self-concept are characterized by behavior including:

- Participating actively

- Independent behavior

- Comfortable having opinions

- Outgoing

- Taking risks

- Positive attitude

- Open to suggestions

- Able to take criticism

Children (and adults) with low self-esteem and a negative self-concept are characterized by behavior including:

- Little participation

- Dependent behavior

- Going along with the crowd

- Introverted behavior

- Fearful behavior

- Negative attitude

- Defensive

As we began to examine the various qualities, characteristics and behaviors that make up this force - self-esteem - a few parents pointed out the fact that so much emphasis both in their upbringing and their children's upbringing has been on productivity - quantity, not quality. We reward the child with straight "A's". We use him as an example for the other children. "Look at the Smith boy. Now he really applies himself. I'm sure he will go to a good college, get a good job, have a beautiful home and family, etc., etc., etc." You may not have spoken these exact words, but probably these thoughts have run through your mind and have been communicated to your children in some way, shape or form.

Let's look at the Smith boy with his straight "A's". First, he is always feeling pressured to keep his perfect record going. Any fluctuation will stimulate feelings of failure. The Smith boy's entire self-image and all of his self-esteem may be wrapped up in his academic record. Does he have friends? Does he consider outside interests and relaxation to be important? Do his parents only appreciate him for his fine academic record? In today's society, even the most successful person, the person in the community with a high powered career and all of the benefits that go along with it, may still be suffering from low self-esteem. After working with many people who have successful careers, I have learned that outer success may have little connection to the inner inadequacies that a person experiences. When you go just below the surface, this person may be filled with feelings with worthlessness. Outer success does not guarantee inner peace.

A number of stay-at-home mothers in the group complained of struggling with low self-esteem problems themselves. They felt looking back that all of their parents' approval (as well as the general reactions around them) came as a result of good grades and specific accomplishments. Their roles as mothers offered none of the reinforcements they had become accustomed to. They felt empty and their self-esteem was evaporating. We must learn to separate the person from his performance. I recall describing people who had impressed me to a very wise mentor. As I listed one accomplishment after another, she looked at me very unimpressed and simply stated, "These are just ornaments on the Christmas tree." I credit her with teaching me the difference between a person's goodness and a person's resume.

A child's level of self-esteem is always changing. Our children are very much influenced by all of the behavior of the significant people in their lives. The self-esteem messages a child receives at home, in school and from peers add up to his feelings about himself.

	High Self-Esteem	**Low Self-Esteem**
Home	"You're a great kid!"	"You're nothing but a big pest!"
School	"You're a pleasure!"	"I've had it with you!"
Peers	"Are you on our team?"	"CREEP. Get lost!"

Exercise:

Completing the following exercises will give you some insight into your child's level of self-esteem and how he may feel about himself. What are some typical messages your child receives in these settings?

At Home:

_____

_____

_____

_____

At School:

_____

_____

_____

_____

From Friends:

_____

_____

_____

_____

The parents in our group had so much to say, we didn't know where to begin. One father told of his adolescent daughter who recently experienced a breakthrough when she got involved in folk dancing, of all things. Here was her claim to fame. Through a local folk dancing group, she was able to connect with peers who not only accepted her, but made her feel special. When his daughter brought this excitement home, tensions in the family began to decrease and grades that were slacking off began to creep up. As parents, we must take on a responsibility to help our children discover a "niche". Adults do this all of the time. We search for a niche in the workplace and in our private lives. You may be involved in a sport, a community organization or a particular social circle. We all search for a feeling of acceptance and belonging. One mother told of her son's success in karate and what an incredible impact it made in all aspects of his life. Children don't have a choice when it comes to going to school, but they do have a choice when it comes to outside activities. Look for your child's special interests or abilities and guide him based on what you see. Remember, outside involvements should be success oriented and fun.

I lecture quite frequently to various community groups. When I make a case for allowing children to come home after school and "chill out",

I see a look of relief on all of the parents' faces. Inevitably, parents will come up to speak with me and telephone me afterwards. "I'm so happy to hear you say that. I feel relieved to know that it's okay for my children to come home and do nothing after school." Did playing go out of style? And what's wrong with a little television? How would you feel after working all day to be rushed off to aerobics, guitar, art lessons, etc.? Wouldn't it just add insult to injury if you just happened to be unathletic, tone deaf and couldn't draw a straight line? Feeling relaxed and loved in the family will ensure more success in life versus an anxious stressed child whose schedule requires an administrative assistant.

School

When it comes to school, parents can and should look into the most appropriate program or classroom for their child. Constant low self-esteem messages from school can indicate that your child is in an inappropriate program (perhaps too difficult or not challenging enough) or he may have a learning disability or learning problem. Many children have struggled for years, feeling like a failure placed in the "low" groups and are the target of teasing from classmates, only to find out that they have a specific learning problem which can be treated. Recently, I met a college sophomore struggling with his academics who sounded as if he had an untreated case of attention deficit disorder. His physician father was never able to admit that his son was imperfect and might benefit from treatment as well as medication. Parents, please get your children the help they need and work through your own difficulties of accepting that your child has a problem.

Pushing your child into a class that is too advanced can be equally damaging. When are we going to accept the fact that most of us are average? One night at dinner, my younger daughter (a middle school student at the time) told me she received a "B" on a social studies test. I know she was waiting for me to ask what kept her from getting an "A". Instead, I bit my tongue and asked, "Are you satisfied with your grade?" She smiled and reminded me sarcastically that "B" was a very satisfactory grade. "After all," she said, "C is average."

Request an evaluation by your school psychologist if you would like an indication of your child's abilities and recommendations for placement. Sometimes, all the tutoring in the world is not what is needed. A number of parents in the group discussed their frustrated efforts at helping their children at home. Of course, many of us review homework, make suggestions, etc. It is when the situation becomes destructive that we have to quit while we are ahead. One mother cried as she told us about the nightly scene after dinner. Each evening the scene escalates to screaming at her daughter and making extremely damaging remarks. "You dummy. You're just not trying. I don't see what is so difficult. We've had it with you. You're making our lives miserable." This mother came to the group looking for new ways to approach her daughter, who at this point was feeling shattered. I have worked with a number of adults who are still healing from the damage done by the negatives messages they received in school and from their families growing up. Seeing themselves as not very smart and not very competent has had a huge impact on many of their life choices.

At any age, how we feel about ourselves will influence all of our thoughts, feelings and behaviors. Building your children's self-esteem is the most effective strategy for helping your children to reach their potential in every aspect of their lives.

QUICK REMINDERS

1. Self-esteem is the sum total of accumulated feelings and evaluations about yourself that add up to your feelings of self-worth.

2. Self-esteem answers the question: How much do I value myself?

3. A child with high self-esteem believes in himself.

4. A child with low self-esteem feels inferior and inadequate.

5. Provide children with time for free play and relaxation.

JOURNAL

What have I learned about my children, my family and myself?

2

SENDING HIGH AND LOW SELF-ESTEEM MESSAGES

> *You are the first person to ever validate me. During my entire life, I have never thought much of myself. I am so used to hearing criticism, so I have spent my life feeling invisible and unimportant. I have felt depressed throughout most of my life, and suffered in silence. This is the first time I am able to assert myself and see who I really am.*
>
> *Joanne, 82-years-old*

Because self-esteem is a dynamic process, it is never too late to change how your children feel about themselves. Joanne, 82, who came to see me after her husband died, is a dramatic example of how the relationships around us and the messages we receive shape our lives. The self-esteem messages we receive from others and send to ourselves influence all of our actions and decisions.

High self-esteem messages nurture relationships and help relationships to grow. A child, or any person for that matter, who is surrounded by these warm, encouraging, supportive, loving messages is more likely to thrive and feel successful. The following are examples of high self-esteem messages:

- Mother: "What a great kid!"

- Father: "I'm so proud to have you as a son!"

- Siblings: "Everybody at school really likes you. "

- Friends: "Fun to be with."

- Teacher: "Very reliable."

On the other hand, when a child is experiencing learning problems, emotional problems, family problems and/or social problems, I guarantee that if you listen carefully you will hear frequent low self-esteem messages coming from several sources. For example:

- Mother: "You have no common sense."

- Father: "You're a real good for nothing!"

- Siblings: "Why can't you be like me?"

- Friends: "You have nothing going for you."

- Teacher: "You make my job miserable."

It is sometimes difficult to determine if the self-esteem messages came before the behavior, or if the behavior results in the self-esteem messages. One parent cited a perfect example of this. For a variety of reasons, her eleven-year-old daughter who was previously struggling academically was transferred into a new, more appropriate academic program. With that, the young girl's status had changed and she was now referred to as "a bright child". Everyone interacted with her differently - her teacher, her parents and her friends. What was the result? With all of these high self-esteem messages, her daughter began to approach everyday with enthusiasm and positive energy. Her performance in school improved dramatically.

On the other hand, this self-fulfilling prophecy works in the other direction. A child who is constantly reminded that she is a troublemaker, a dummy, classroom clown or a real pain in the neck also rises to the occasion. This child often will do everything to prove you are right. She won't read. She will disturb an entire classroom of children. As she gets older, she may become a menace in your community, get involved with drugs and alcohol or develop other problems.

We all love to hear the positive but it is unrealistic to think that everything will always flow in that direction. Certainly, all children receive both high and low self-esteem messages from their families, in school and from their friends.

High Self-Esteem Messages:

- Smiles and hugs.

- Home: "I love you."

- Peers: "I would like to be friends with you."

- School: "We want you to be on our team."

Low Self-Esteem Messages:

- Frowns.

- Home: "You're not going to school looking like that."

- Peers: "Get lost."

- School: "If you were paying attention, you would know what we are doing."

Give some thought to the high self-esteem and low self-esteem messages your children experience from day to day.

High Self-Esteem Messages:

- "You're very good at that!"

- "I enjoy being with you."

- "You make me so proud of you."

- "Didn't we have fun together?"

- Phone calls from friends.

- Invitations to birthday parties and other events.

17

- Happy faces, stars, etc. on school papers.

- Feeling listened to.

- "Let's plan something special."

- "You've made so much progress."

- "You're such a great person."

- "You put a lot of effort into that."

Low Self-Esteem Messages:

- "I'm not happy with you."

- "You are so lazy."

- "You are so small for your age."

- "You're such a baby."

- No phone calls – no invitations.

- Large black X's and slashes all over school papers.

- Dirty looks and being ignored.

- "Why don't you do something constructive?"

- "You have no direction!"

- "You never accomplish anything."

- "Can't you brush your hair?"

- "What happened to your grades? Your brother did much better than that."

- "We don't want you in our play!"

- "Do I have to sit next to her?"

- "Why can't you be like everyone else?"

Can you think of any others?

High Self-Esteem Messages:

_____

_____

_____

_____

Low Self-Esteem Messages:

_____

_____

_____

_____

Be An Advocate

Let's not kid ourselves. All of us send low self-esteem messages to our children at various times. It is a question of how much they have to hear these messages. It is impossible to dictate to our children's teachers and our children's friends the messages they are sending to our children. In essence, there are times we have to roll with the punches. On the other hand, I see nothing wrong with a parent intervening on her child's behalf. In fact, I encourage you to be an advocate for your children. Meet with a teacher to hear the facts and to see if some of the difficulties can be resolved. Share your side of the story and work as a team. For some reason, many parents are hesitant to contact a child's teacher. Some say they don't want to make a big issue out of a situation. Others say they will wait until parent conferences or wait for the teacher to contact them. I disagree. This is your child. Express your interest and concern directly to the teacher. Don't wait for anything. Two heads are always better than one. Your child will respond to the fact that you and the teacher are collaborating as a team. Consider a teacher who becomes angry with a child for not paying attention on a daily basis. Perhaps a change at home is distracting the child, such as a move to a new house, a grandparent who has moved in with the family or a recent separation or divorce. It could be any number of things. Meeting with a child's teacher opens the lines of communication. I'm often amazed at how little contact takes place between parents and the adult(s) who are responsible for their children six hours per day, five days per week, forty weeks per year. Never hesitate to make a phone call or set up a meeting. Just a few minutes of discussion can make all the difference in the world for your child.

The same goes for your child's relationships with friends. Children, unfortunately, can get out of hand with cruel remarks. Why should your child suffer unnecessarily? Often, a call to the school or to a friend's parent will shed some light on a situation. If your child's behavior is part of the problem, once you know the facts, you may be able to help her to change her behavior and the situation. One mother talked of her son's recent experience in a pre-school summer camp at a local park. Her son was excluded from many activities, and in general had a very negative experience. Only weeks later did she find out the root of the problem. Due to an allergic reaction, her son had a skin rash on his hands that looked awful. At that age, many activities require picking a partner and holding hands with your partner. All of the children began to notice the rash and reacted with shrieks, "yucks", etc. None of the other children wanted him as a partner. He was often chosen last for activities, and of course, he felt rejected. A quick phone call might have alerted the counselor to handle the situation differently. Don't wait until a situation is out of control. It is your right as a parent to call a teacher, a counselor, a coach, a dance or music instructor or a friend's family to express concern and interest to resolve the problem at hand.

In order to help us experience first hand the feelings of a child bombarded with high self-esteem messages and the feelings of a child bombarded with low self-esteem messages, our parent group began reflecting on our own life experiences. We listened to examples of our parents' interactions with us from elementary school through the present. Needless to say, the feelings raised ranged from joy to deep sadness, making this a difficult exercise for many people.

Exercise:

Think about your life and the messages (both verbal and non-verbal) you have received from your parents.

What messages did you receive and do you presently receive from your parents that boost your self-esteem?

_____

_____

_____

_____

What messages did you receive and do you presently receive from your parents that erode your self-esteem?

_____

_____

_____

_____

What was really striking in our group was how many moments from the past we were able to recall so vividly. This exercise will help you to fully appreciate how powerful the impact of our actions and behaviors are on our children. This is a tremendous responsibility that we need to take seriously at all times. As the parent of adult children, I continue to observe how important my reactions are to my two daughters. I remind myself often to choose my words carefully and continue to practice all of the skills presented in this book.

A steady diet of low self-esteem messages can affect a child's behavior at home, at school and with her peers. Consider each of us to possess a certain amount of energy, which we must divide among our various activities, relationships and involvements. If I had to make one general statement about low self-esteem messages, I would say that they drain your energy. A child has very little, if any, energy left over to learn or to interact with others in healthy relationships.

- *Low self-esteem messages drain your energy.*

- *High self-esteem messages replenish your energy.*

Focusing On Strengths

Focusing on each family member's unique "specialness" is vital in order to make each person feel valued. When we feel important and appreciated for who we are, our self-esteem increases. I asked group members to make a list of behaviors, qualities and strengths they liked about their children. I suggested that we go around the group and share one or two of the items about each child. The most dramatic effect took place with each and every person around the room. Regardless of the child being discussed, there was a pride, a warmth and a deep love that emerged everywhere. You could feel it and you certainly could see it.

> *"My daughter may have had her problems, but I must say she is courageous. It has been her courage that kept her going and trying out new situations."*
>
> *"His sense of humor is contagious."*
>
> *"I have never seen such a good-natured child."*

When you identify the positive qualities of a person, your energy will always shift. Looking for the positive will help you, particularly when the going gets rough. Certainly, when conflicts and problems develop, it is easy for the list of strengths to vanish. For that reason, I suggest keeping a running list posted on the refrigerator. Acknowledging and simply remembering what you like about each child will have a definite impact on your behavior as a parent.

A grandfather called me to discuss his adolescent granddaughter on my radio show one day. He complained and complained about her attitude, her lateness and her fresh talk to her mother. While venting negative feelings is important, I felt his escalating anger was not productive. Before I commented on his anger, I simply asked, "What do you like about her?" There was a hesitation for a few seconds. The man that responded at that point had very little likeness to the man who was initially expressing the angry tirade. One of the beauties of radio is that so much is communicated by tone of voice. This grandfather began to list attributes about his granddaughter he found likeable. Actually, he sounded shocked listening to himself. This happens so often to all of us. We become so problem oriented. So critical. How easy it is to forget that every child possesses likeable qualities.

Exercise:

Make a list of the behaviors/qualities/strengths you like about each member of your immediate family.

Child: _____

    1. _____

    2. _____

    3. _____

    4. _____

Child: _____

    1. _____

    2. _____

    3. _____

    4. _____

Child: _____

    1. _____

    2. _____

    3. _____

    4. _____

Child: _____

    1. _____

    2. _____

    3. _____

    4. _____

Partner: _____

    1. _____

    2. _____

    3. _____

    4. _____

What qualities do you value about yourself?

_____

_____

_____

_____

Recognizing these qualities is a step in the right direction. Communicating these feelings directly (through a statement or gesture) is even better. Remember, high self-esteem messages nurture relationships and help them to grow.

Even the well intentioned parent communicates verbal as well as nonverbal messages to their children that, at times, are damaging to their self-esteem. The result? GUILT. "I did the wrong thing" plays over and over in our minds. Avoid the guilt trap. Instead, focus on your awareness to help you in the future. Learning from our mistakes, accepting them and forgiving ourselves is healing. It is the best way to let go and move forward. Parenthood is a teaching relationship. We are teaching our children lessons about the real world, including the fact that everyone makes mistakes and no one is expected to be perfect. Always keep in mind that there are no perfect parents.

The Goal Is Change

My goal in writing this book is to help you to change your behavior. After all, the bottom line is change. For many of us, change is frightening and can be threatening. To change often makes us feel that we have been doing it wrong. Not true. To change is to grow and to learn from your experiences. People change, children change and situations change. All of the changes need not come from you. It is overwhelming and unrealistic to believe that everything your child is and everything your child does is a reflection of you. It is often difficult to accept a child as a separate person with her own unique attributes, strengths and weaknesses.

I encourage you as you read this book to continue to reflect on your child's strengths. I say this because this book is a process. As we participate in this process together, you may see different strengths and new strengths both in your child and yourself. Recognizing these strengths will be reflected in your behavior and will help to build self-esteem. Think about the positive self-esteem messages you have received in your life that have made the most impact on you. What did they communicate to you?

- Acceptance?
- Competence?
- Unconditional love?
- Appreciation?
- Pride?

Are you communicating these feelings to your children? How are you communicating these feelings to your children?

For Practice:

1. Using your list of special qualities, practice sending messages to family members, acknowledging their unique specialness.

2. Listen for high and low self-esteem messages in the family, at work and in social situations.

QUICK REMINDERS

1. Self-esteem is the sum total of accumulated feelings and evaluations about yourself that add up to your sense of self-worth.

2. Self-esteem is a dynamic ever-changing process.

3. High self-esteem messages nurture relationships and help relationships grow.

4. Low self-esteem messages limit growth and are more frequent in troubled relationships.

5. Let each family member know (often) how special he/she is through a statement or a gesture.

6. There are no perfect parents!

JOURNAL

What have I learned about my children, my family and myself?

3

UNDERSTANDING THE FAMILY SYSTEM

I was always seen as the problem child in my family and at school. My parents sent me to a therapist for years, hoping I would straighten out. Now that I am an adult and have a family of my own, I understand that in many ways I was the scapegoat for many problems in my family that had nothing to do with me. It has taken me years for me to feel that I am not a horrible person.

Jim, Father of 2

In order to fully understand your child, you must have an understanding of the workings of what we call "the family system." No one exists in isolation. Each of us participates in an intricate web of relationships. Problems, conflicts and situations that merit our attention often exist in the interactions between people. They do not belong to just one person. For instance, consider Mike, a five-year-old boy, who is coming home from school crying for the last six months. Some might react to him in the following fashion:

- "Stop being a crybaby. Grow up!"

- "Send him to the school psychologist."

- "Give him this medication."

All three of these reactions place all of the responsibility for the problem and the responsibility for change on the boy's shoulders. These reactions also are filled with blame, which often leads to guilt. All three reactions contain undertones of: "There's something wrong with you."

Looking through a "family systems lens" you would see something very different from the above description. The family system is defined by all of the relationships this family participates in, including the immediate and extended families, work relationships, the relationships at school, the relationships in the community, and the family's relationship with the norms of today's society. In order to examine all of the facets and forces at work here, we need to find out who is in the family system. Here are a few questions we can ask:

1. Who are the close family members in the family, including parents, grandparents and ex-spouses and their families?

2. Who are the significant teachers, staff and students the child and the family deal with at school?

3. Who do the parents encounter each day at work?

4. What are the stresses in the community and cultural group(s) this family is part of?

5. What pressures of contemporary society affect this family?

Mike's Family System

In the case of our five-year-old boy, let's begin by looking at the immediate family:

Dad: Dave, 35-years-old   Mom: Angie, 30-years-old

Child: Mike, 5-years-old   Child: Carol, 12-months-old

Now, let's take a closer look at Mike's family system. Angie and Dave were married seven years ago. At that time, they were both involved in their careers and Angie was earning slightly more than Dave. They had a large circle of friends and a wide variety of interests. After Mike was born, Angie returned to work part-time. Although their lifestyle as a couple changed to meet the needs of the baby, they were able to continue somewhat of a social life with the help of Angie's parents on the weekends. Dave's parents live four hours away by car, and were able to help out during occasional visits. During the next few years, Dave was promoted several times and is presently a vice president of his company. Although Angie and Dave have become more comfortable financially, Angie is not thrilled with Dave's long hours. Dave works in a very competitive field where long hours are the norm. He appears preoccupied with business matters and has developed a short fuse at home. Last year, Angie gave birth to Carol and decided to leave her job for the time being. Taking care of two children turned out to be considerably more demanding than having one child. Angie's parents have since retired and moved to another part of the country, making it more difficult to get out on the weekends with Dave. Dave has taken on several new projects, and is traveling on a regular basis, leaving Angie with the majority of the responsibility for the children and their home.

Mike attended pre-school and kindergarten and enjoyed both experiences. Now that he has entered first grade, his behavior is beginning to change. He is finding learning to read extremely difficult. Dave does not understand the problem and is beginning to criticize Angie for being too focused on the new baby. If she gave Mike more attention, he wouldn't be having these difficulties. Mike's teacher mentioned something about a special program for him, but both Dave and Angie were appalled at the thought. With all of the responsibilities and demands of a first grade class, Mike's reading problems have been slipping between the cracks. Several of Mike's classmates are teasing him about his difficulties reading. Mike is coming off of the school bus crying several times each week. Angie, busy with the baby, distracts Mike with an entertaining afternoon children's television show.

Here are some questions to think about:

Q. Is this only Mike's problem?

Mike's behavior is extremely visible and easy to focus on, but it seems as though Dave and Angie are hurting as well. Dave is angry and frustrated. Angie is feeling depressed and isolated.

Q. How has Mike's self-esteem changed during the last few years?
With the birth of the baby, Mike has certainly been "dethroned". Wherever he goes with his mother and the baby, everyone makes a fuss about baby Carol. It seems that the high self-esteem messages Mike was accustomed to receiving are primarily going to the baby. His mom seems terribly busy and is short-tempered with him. The same is true for his father. They often send low self-esteem messages like:

- "You're a big boy now, stop acting like a baby."

- "Leave your mother alone. She's busy with the baby."

- "Don't make Dad angry. He's tired from work."

Q. What changes have taken place in the family system?
Grandma and Grandpa made Mike feel special, but now they're far away. Although they telephone often, Mike misses all of the afternoons he used to spend with them. School has become a lot more difficult. Mike's teacher makes funny faces at him when he doesn't understand the directions. Even some of his friends are reacting to him differently and sometimes giggling when Mike doesn't understand the class work. The bombardment of low self-esteem messages from all parts of the family system is destroying Mike's self-esteem.

Q. Has the marital relationship been affected by all of the changes?
Angie and Dave are feeling the tension. They are experiencing the stress of a new baby. They are upset about Mike's difficulties in school. In general, they are left with little time and energy to enjoy each other. Lately, Dave feels less anxious to hurry home from the office or a business trip. Home just is not the relaxing place it used to be.

Q. Has Angie's self-esteem been affected by all of the changes?
Since Angie left her job, she has less social contact and no paycheck. She no longer receives the high self-esteem messages from her colleagues and her accomplishments on the job. Angie's parents are

no longer available for support and social contact. They, too, were a source of high self-esteem messages. Dave has been more critical lately, sending her low self-esteem messages on a regular basis. In addition, he has had considerably less time for Angie, which has had a powerful effect on Angie's self-esteem.

Q. Has Dave's self-esteem been affected by all of the changes?
Dave has certainly been moving fast in the company. His self-esteem at work is at an all time high. On the other hand, he and Angie have been bickering so often lately. Although he knows he's doing his best at home, he is beginning to feel inadequate as a husband. He often wonders why Angie seems so unhappy.

Whose Problem Is It?

As you can see, when one person in the family has developed a problem, it is an absolute necessity to examine the entire family system. This way you can begin to intervene in different parts of the system in order to create changes. In the case of Mike's family, although the "identified patient" is Mike, everyone is part of the problem, and everyone must be part of the solution. Effective strategies for change include couples counseling for Angie and Dave and planning an appropriate reading program to address Mike's difficulties.

If your child is developing a problem, examine your family system to uncover the relationships that may be contributing to the difficulties. Understanding your family system will help you to unravel the underlying problems that may be affecting your child's self-esteem. This will help you to plan effective strategies for improving your child's self-esteem.

The Family System

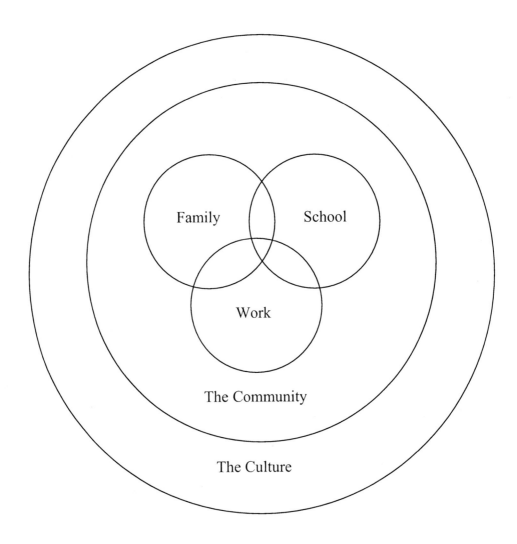

Watching For Changes In The Family System

When examining the family system, watch for changes in any of the family member's behavior. The changes in one person's behavior "ripple" throughout the system. When a child develops a problem, it may be a consequence of a change or stress occurring in some part of the family system. Any change or transition can result in the formation of a problem for someone in the family.

A child will react to:

- A new baby
- Changes in caregivers
- Rejection by peers
- A new school or a new teacher
- More difficult academic work
- Difficulties in a teacher's personal life
- Entering adolescence
- Changes in extracurricular programs
- Loss of a friend
- Illness
- Death
- Parent taking new job
- Changes in parent's work schedule
- Parent's depression or anxiety
- Parent's "mid-life crisis"
- Marital stress

- Changes in financial status

- Family move

- Divorce

- Re-marriage

- Addition of stepchildren to the family

I'm sure you have experienced many changes not on this list. Again, a child will react (as will all family members) to any change in the family system. Who isn't stressed during times of transition and change? If you think it is difficult to send high self-esteem messages in the family, just wait for a period of change. Most of us turn into somebody else when the pressure is on. Unfortunately, it is during these times of change that our children need us more than ever. During these stressful periods you may find yourself making statements like:

- "Leave me alone!"

- "What do you want from me?"

- "Can't you see I have a lot on my mind?"

- "Don't disturb Mom/Dad. She/he is upset."

- "Why are you doing this to me?"

When a child receives so many of these messages from everyone who is important to him, self-esteem is at risk.

How Problems Develop

A child bombarded with low self-esteem messages from all sides will, sooner or later, develop a problem. It often begins with a small problem and mushrooms into something more complicated. What do I mean by a problem? Here are the more common problems that children develop:

- Excessive crying and whining
- Aggressive behavior
- Bedwetting
- Biting
- Eating (too little or too much)
- Sleeping problems
- Lying
- Easily frustrated
- Teasing others and bullying
- Victim of teasing and bullying
- Poor attention span
- Inability to read
- Low or failing grades
- Fighting (verbally or physically)
- Socially withdrawn
- Some speech problems
- School phobia
- Perfectionism
- Expecting too much from self
- Lack of confidence
- Depression
- Anxiety
- Fears
- Nightmares

- Sibling rivalry

- Overly concerned about physical appearance

- Drug/alcohol abuse

- Cutting

- Sexual promiscuity

- Running away

- Constant anger/hostility

- Dropping out of school

- Inability to hold a job

- Difficulty moving out of home (at an appropriate age)

This list may seem overwhelming! Although most children experience problems from time to time, the intensity and duration of these problems vary greatly. Understanding self-esteem, self-esteem messages and the role of the family system will empower you when you see a problem beginning to develop.

Although all families send low self-esteem messages to their children at times, does that mean that all families will experience these problems? Yes and no. I firmly believe that all families have problems. You may not see this at first glance unless you look beneath the surface. For some reason, many of us feel it is necessary to wear a smile and spread the word that everything is great. How unreal, isolating and lonely. When you think about the family system and all of the people, all of the relationships, and all of the emotion, how could everything run smoothly all of the time?

Granted, there are times when there is no one available to confide in. I do feel, though, that often we just don't want others to be aware of our pain. Perhaps no one has expressed any interest in our pain. If you don't have a good friend who will listen and understand, connect with a therapist who will, or join a support group for people with similar struggles. I often urge clients I speak with on a weekly basis to become involved in a support group with people who may be experiencing a similar situation. Any group of parents with a commitment to learning and growing together will prove to be an incredible asset in your life. When I began my career, I facilitated my first parent group at a local YWCA. As a group, we represented a variety of backgrounds and ages. Our children ranged from 2-22 and our concerns were very different. When our ten-week contract expired, the group decided to meet in each other's homes and the meetings continued for six years. I continue to run into group members in my community and am often reminded of the incredible network of support and relationships that evolved for these parents. Consider organizing an ongoing parent group in your community using this book as a springboard for discussion. The group experience is extremely powerful and supportive.

Existing Problems Lead To Low Self-Esteem Messages

We have established the fact that low self-esteem messages can lead to problems. It works in the other direction as well. Existing problems that we have no control over can mushroom into multi-layered problems when a child is bombarded with low self-esteem messages. Consider a child with:

- Physical or mental challenges

- Learning disabilities

- Attention deficit disorder

- Speech problems

- Medical problems

- Advanced intellectual abilities

One mother in our group cried as she described the cruel treatment her dyslexic son received at school and in the neighborhood. The same is true of a physical challenge. A mother whose son was born with a birth defect recently phoned me with horror stories regarding her son's experiences in second grade. Even when there is an existing problem not necessarily related to low self-esteem, low self-esteem messages sent by parents, school and friends lead to the development of a new layer of problems. For this reason, it is certainly not unusual for a child with a learning disability, a physical challenge or medical condition to also have related emotional problems. Who wouldn't? Often, these self-esteem problems go unaddressed. The child is offered tutoring, a special class or proper medical treatment, but what about his self-esteem? What are we doing to rebuild his self-esteem?

Your Family System

Take a few moments to examine your family system. Who are the significant people in each part of your family system?

Family:

_____

_____

_____

_____

School/Child's Daily Routine:

_____

_____

_____

_____

Work:

_____

_____

_____

_____

What messages or forces in your community affect your day-to-day life?

_____

_____

_____

_____

What messages in our culture affect your day-to-day life?

_____

_____

_____

_____

QUICK REMINDERS

1. It is important to understand your family system. Your family system is made up of members of your immediate and extended families, your relationships at work and the relationships that impact your child's daily life. All of these relationships function within the context of your individual community as well as today's society.

2. Many problems and conflicts exist in the interaction between members of the family system.

3. When one member of the family develops a problem, examine the entire family system in order to plan strategies for change.

4. Change and transitions are stressful. Any change for one member of the family can ripple through the entire family system and affect a child's behavior.

JOURNAL

What have I learned about my children, my family and myself?

_____

_____

_____

_____

_____

_____

_____

_____

_____

_____

_____

_____

_____

_____

_____

_____

_____

_____

_____

4

IS ANYONE LISTENING ?

When someone is listening, we feel valued.

When was the last time you really felt someone was listening to you? Feeling listened to is an incredibly high-powered self-esteem message. When someone really listens to you, the message you receive is:

- "I think you're important."

- "I care about you."

- "I understand you."

- "I am able to put my feelings and opinions aside long enough to be aware of yours."

When you feel listened to, you feel validated. Many of us live with a tremendous amount of self-doubt because the important people in our lives won't listen to us. Instead, they may bombard us with low self-esteem messages like:

- "Are you crazy?"

- "What do you mean by that?"

- "That's ridiculous."

- Ignoring us.

- Avoiding us.

- No eye contact.

- Attempting to listen while busy with many other things.

When you receive messages like these, expressing yourself becomes more and more difficult. When no one will listen, we feel:

- Alone

- Depressed

- Angry

- Neglected

- Worthless

- Disappointed

- Unimportant

- Frustrated

- Hurt

- Useless

- Rejected

When the people who are most important to you accept your feelings and thoughts, you feel better about yourself. The feeling you walk away with is:

- ***"I'm okay. There's nothing wrong with me. No one is going to reject me because of the way I feel."***

Can you think of a time in your life you wished someone important in your life communicated that feeling to you?

_____

_____

_____

_____

Unspoken Rules of Communication

It is not uncommon for families to have unspoken rules where many feelings are off limits. For instance, you may be able to communicate warmth or approval freely, but don't even consider expressing your anger. On the other hand, in many families anger and conflict are the norm but caring and acceptance are out of the question. Whatever the combination, most families give the green light to certain feelings while other feelings are unacceptable.

Think about your present family and the family you grew up in. Make a list of permissible feelings.

_____

_____

_____

_____

Make a list of those feelings that are off limits in your present family and the family you grew up in.

_____

_____

_____

_____

How do we handle this set of unspoken rules? Often, adults will reach out to someone outside of the immediate family to vent their "unacceptable" feelings. A woman will confide in her best friend. A man will speak to a friend or colleague. We may involve a mother, father or in-law. Acting out is often a response to not feeling free to express feelings at home. If we don't find someone who will listen, we may become depressed, lonely, isolated, or angry. A child who acts out may be a child who has no one in the family system who will listen to her. A child who develops emotional or behavioral problems may be a child who has no one who will listen. Listening diffuses tension and pressure. Feeling listened to brings on a sense of relief.

Special Programs For Listening

Circle time in pre-schools and elementary schools is a structured activity that gives teachers an opportunity to listen to children's thoughts, feelings and concerns. Each child is asked to share anything that is on her mind. Many problem situations are identified by skilled staff who are trained to listen and observe both verbal and nonverbal behavior. Teachers listen for changes in the family system, and use this information to engage parents in a dialogue. During circle time, a teacher may hear statements that reveal a depressed or anxious child or a child who is reaching out for help. I have worked with many parents who have received valuable feedback from teachers as a result of circle time.

Several years ago, I was involved in establishing a telephone hotline for area teens. At a meeting introducing the hotline to local professionals, I was challenged by one gentleman. He could not understand the value of a telephone call (often the caller chose to stay anonymous) without ongoing treatment. Here is where we each have to recall a time when a phone call or conversation with someone who listened helped us though a particularly difficult moment. When someone calls a hotline in crisis, there is someone on the other end who will respond at a time when the caller feels there is absolutely no one who cares. The power of feeling listened to can prevent someone from taking that next drink, getting high, screaming at a child, hitting a child or attempting suicide. Listening creates a connection between two people.

Peer counseling is a program that responds to the child who needs someone to talk to. Many schools, middle and senior high schools as well as colleges, are establishing peer counseling programs in order to respond to students who need someone to talk to. Peer counselors are volunteers who are trained and supervised by a professional. Students are made aware of the peer counselors and are urged to contact one if they have any problems related to school, home or relationships. The meetings typically take place informally after school. I had the opportunity to interview several groups of peer counselors and students who feel they have been helped through peer counseling. The program is successful because the students feel listened to. "She really knew what I was going through" was an expression I heard over and over again. Several college students expressed less willingness to speak to a professional because they felt professionals can be distant and less real. Certainly, the average teen will seek out a peer long before she will seek out an adult. Guidance counselors state that many students who otherwise would not reach out for help are being helped tremendously. Furthermore, the peer counselors know who needs help because they listen. They listen at parties, in the hallways, and they listen to other students' behavior. If your community does not have a peer-counseling program, I encourage you to begin one.

Is Anyone In The Family System Listening?

When a child feels that no one in the family system will listen, self-esteem goes down the drain. Effective listening is one of the most powerful high self-esteem messages a child can receive. Let me share with you a few examples of children who could not find anyone to listen.

I recently addressed a group of parents in an upper middle-class community. My lecture consisted of many of the points in this book and was entitled "Building Your Child's Self-Esteem." The lecture was well attended by parents of children of all ages. One week later, I received a phone call from a mother who attended the lecture. She explained that her twelve-year-old daughter had swallowed a number of aspirins in an attempt to commit suicide approximately four months ago. I gathered some information on the telephone and set up an appointment to meet with the parents. At my initial meeting with the parents, I gathered information about the family system. I noticed both parents were concerned, but, at the same time, they were minimizing the severity of the problem. The mother (a nurse) assured me that the number of aspirins her daughter swallowed could not have killed her. Denial is an incredibly strong obstacle to listening. I inquired about changes in the family system and was told that no major changes had taken place in the last year. I did get the impression that the girl's younger siblings were a problem. The family seemed to be organized around the twin pre-schoolers, with the twelve-year-old feeling pushed aside. Again, I was assured this was not a problem for the girl. It seemed that the parents made no connection between the girl's behavior and the behavior of the family system. No one was listening to this girl's cries for help. Her parents saw her physical appearance go down the drain. They complained that her room was so filthy, they couldn't even walk in. But, again, they were not listening to these behaviors.

I met the girl the following week and it was obvious that she felt relief to finally have someone who would listen. She lost her best friend about eight months ago when a third neighborhood girl came between them. I experienced her deep sense of loss as I listened to the description of their time spent together and the best friend charms they both wore. Her attachment to this girl was central in her life. I made a mental note that when asked what changes had occurred in the girl's life, her parents couldn't think of a thing. This young girl was grieving alone. It was obvious that she found her parents to be unavailable emotionally. As I listened from week to week, I saw some definite changes in the girl's behavior. She began to take more time with her appearance. She seemed less depressed and had more energy and willingness to look at the possibility of making some new friends. I listened as she grieved for the old friend. She began to talk of a new girlfriend, and within several weeks came in wearing a best friend charm they purchased together at a local shopping mall. I decided to bring her parents into the counseling sessions. After all, she wanted so desperately for them to listen to her. More than likely, I moved too fast because her parents were finding it almost impossible to listen and continued to be terribly defensive. I heard low self-esteem messages like:

- "I've tried to be a good mother."

- "I've failed as a parent."

- "We give her everything."

- "Your younger siblings are crazy about you."

- "When I was your age . . ."

They would not listen. It appeared that listening would be some form of admitting that they were wrong. Unfortunately, within a few weeks the family stopped coming. My request to listen to their daughter was too uncomfortable, and was asking them to change too many of their present beliefs and patterns. In retrospect, I should have continued to work individually with the girl. She was doing well, and I should have continued to listen to her. If I had been listening more effectively, I'm sure I would have heard her parents' unwillingness to participate at this time. Expecting too much is a form of not listening and diminishes self-esteem. I expected too much change from this family system. I would like to add that these were good people who, obviously, had more stresses in their family system than I was aware of. They wanted me to help their daughter, but were not ready to accept help for themselves.

Another situation I found particularly striking involved a mother who was referred to me by the school guidance counselor. Her eleven-year-old daughter (a sixth grader) was receiving C and D grades after being an A and B student for years. The girl was becoming more withdrawn, and beginning to put up a fuss about going to school. When I met the mother, I learned that her daughter had experienced an accident in gym last year and was operated on last spring. Six months later, something in her foot had not healed properly, and her daughter was still on crutches and in pain. Apparently, the other students were teasing her about the accident, sending low-esteem messages like:

- "Baby."

- "Faker."

- Mimicking the girl's complaints.

Her teachers (there was a team of four teachers) also refused to listen. One teacher often stated, "You don't look like you're in pain." The girl was quiet, shy, and making the best of the situation. No one was listening and she was suffering.

I made contact with the orthopedic surgeon (remember to consider all members of the family system) and she confirmed that the girl's pain was legitimate. In fact, she had several phone conversations with the school nurse about the situation and was surprised that the teachers had not been more supportive. I made a visit to the school and met with the team of teachers and explained my role with the family. I listened to the teachers defend the grades they had given to the girl. Their nonverbal behavior (facial gestures and tones of voice) were especially angry. I asked that they give her some support in the way of acknowledging her pain and discomfort. The teachers were incredibly resistant. They wouldn't listen to me, but suggested that something from the physician in writing might aid in their understanding of the situation. I phoned the surgeon and she quickly sent a letter directly to the team of teachers explaining and confirming the girl's pain. Within the next few weeks, the girl reported that her teachers began to send high self-esteem messages like:

- "You're working hard."

- "How are you feeling?"

- "Do you need any help?"

- "Nice to see you."

Her teachers interceded if they heard any teasing from other students. Slowly, her grades took a turn and she was receiving B's and C's. Her mother came in thrilled one day and told me, "I feel like I'm getting my daughter back." In June, the guidance counselor who referred the family called to tell me that the girl received a great improvement award at the end of the year assembly. Although we have a happy ending here, I can't believe the effort that went into getting someone to listen to this young girl. I immediately think of the scores of children who don't have anyone to advocate for them!

Is Your Partner Listening?

Certainly, when parents refuse to listen to each other, a child's self-esteem is affected. Arguing, conflict and tension interfere with the energy a parent has to listen to a child. If you are experiencing a great deal of conflict with your partner, do everyone in the family a favor and arrange to meet with a couples counselor. In counseling, you can improve and build a more fulfilling relationship. If you have a specific time and place in which to work out your difficulties, you won't be tied up in knots every second at home. A parent who is preoccupied, aggravated or depressed is not in a position to listen to a child.

Time Out For Listening

Time plays a significant role in your ability to listen. With many people today juggling a number of roles, it is often difficult to find a few free, unscheduled minutes. If this is the case, I suggest you write down your daily schedule and re-evaluate your priorities. There is nothing more valuable to a child than TIME. A parent who has no time and is always on the run can't listen and is sending a low self-esteem message to their children on a consistent basis:

- *"I don't value you."*

A young woman who was incredibly involved in community affairs came to see me because of the overwhelming stress she was experiencing. While I felt that her work was admirable, she had almost no time for her young demanding children. In her defense she exclaimed, "It really gets to me, because I'm doing this all for the kids." While I realize it is important to keep your life interesting, I often feel we may be running away from something if it becomes vital to fill up every minute of everyday. This was certainly the case in this situation. The marriage was really falling apart and this woman's method of coping was running as fast as she possibly could. If this sounds like you, don't run away from the feelings, confront them. A parent on the run can't stand still long enough to interact with her children. In addition, the stress of taking on too much will definitely catch up with you.

Eye Contact Says You're Important

Eye contact is vital when you are listening to your child. Because so much of our messages are communicated nonverbally, you will miss the true meaning of what is said if you are not maintaining any eye contact. Eye contact, in itself, is an incredibly strong high self-esteem message. When you look at a person who is speaking to you, you are saying:

- "You are important."

- "What you are saying is important to me."

- "I am interested in you."

- "I accept you."

Eye contact will help to develop a closer relationship with your child. Eye contact is a way of increasing intimacy between people, that special closeness we may have with those who are important to us. Intimacy is not automatic in a family. You have to work toward it. Many of us have learned to keep our distance from one another and eye contact removes these boundaries. I can't tell you how much you will be able to learn if you look in a child's eyes when she is talking. You will be able to read the feelings behind the words - the true art of listening. Use yourself as a thermostat. When speaking to your child, let your body register the emotional temperature coming from your child. See what feelings register for you. Be a mirror for her. If you feel confused, she's confused. If you feel nervous, she's nervous. This takes practice! It takes a great deal of self-control to simply LISTEN, and not react. If you are always reacting, you are not listening.

Set The Mood To Listen

You have to set the mood for listening. Get rid of all of the distractions: the computer, the phone, the newspaper, the television, and free yourself from other conversations. Make yourself physically available. The parents in our group made a commitment to listen to each child for fifteen minutes each day. This may sound like a meager gesture, but, for many of us, this fifteen minutes takes planning and effort. It is important to devote a separate fifteen minutes to each child. Many parents suggest staggering bedtimes slightly so that each child receives some separate time. Although we often count the minutes to bedtime so we can put our feet up, I do feel it will be to your benefit to stagger the bedtimes slightly. If nothing else, it makes the older child feel special (a high self-esteem message) which will help to diffuse some feelings of rivalry with the younger children.

Roadblocks to Listening

There are many obstacles to effective listening. Let me describe some of the more common roadblocks I observe both professionally as well as in social situations.

- **Interrupting**

Give your child the space to complete her thought. I can guarantee you that you will never hear what your child intended to tell you if you are an interrupter. Even if your child seems to be having a tough time, practice self-restraint and give her the time she needs to sort out her feelings and thoughts. As far as you are concerned, the less said the better. Remember, you are supposed to be listening.

- **Thinking Ahead**

It is so annoying to speak to someone that is thinking ahead of you. If you improve your eye contact it might be easier to stay at the same pace as the person speaking to you. If you are one or two steps ahead of the person you are talking with, you are definitely not listening.

- **Taking Away Feelings**

"That's not true" is a phrase I hear over and over again in so many families. If a child expresses a feeling to you, this feeling is true for her. You may feel hurt, confused or angry about what you are hearing, but you can't take it away. The real problem is within you. You may want to control the situation. The situation may be uncomfortable but listening is the first step towards change. Change will create a situation that is more satisfying to everyone in the family.

Listening To Nonverbal Behavior

Listening to nonverbal behavior (facial expressions, tone of voice, gestures) may be even more important than listening to the words spoken. Experts in the field state that 90% of the message is reflected in nonverbal behavior. Of course, this makes eye contact vital. We want to hear the feelings behind the words because so often the words are not an accurate means of understanding a situation. Often, we will mask our true feelings and bury them in words. I remember once in graduate school volunteering for a role-play with my professor. She engaged me in a dialogue about a problem I was having. As I became more nervous and more defensive, I became wordier and wordier. After allowing me to ramble in circles for at least twenty minutes, she gently said, "You sound very unhappy." The words were so simple, but, honestly, I could not say them out loud. One only had to watch the expression on my face to see that I was attempting to talk my unhappiness away.

Being sidetracked by someone's words is a common problem. Now, I am not suggesting that there is a conspiracy going on to get you off the right track. Often we are not in touch with our true feelings. In addition, many of us are experts at fooling ourselves. We know how we feel, but we tell ourselves some other truth, and then go around repeating it. Why? Maybe we are afraid of the reaction we will get. Remember, in most families certain feelings are off limits. If you are listening carefully to the nonverbal behavior, you will be more likely to hear the true message. I suggest you check out your thoughts and help to clarify your child's feelings. Don't assume anything. Use statements like:

- "You look upset. . .." (Wait for a response)

- "You look disappointed. . . ." (Wait for a response)

The goal is <u>NOT</u> to be right or wrong. The goal is to open up discussion. Perhaps you say to your child, "You look upset," and she responds, "No, I have a sore throat and couldn't get my work done in school. I don't feel well." We get ourselves into big trouble assuming we know what other people are thinking. This is a huge problem with many families I work with.

Trust Is A High Self-Esteem Message

Trust is an incredibly important component to listening. A child needs to trust that a parent will be there if she is to ask you to listen. Many parents feel that trust should be automatic. "After all, I'm her mother." Sorry, it doesn't work like that. Just as trust is built within any adult relationship, trust must also be built in a parent/child relationship. A parent who is consistent and dependable will win a child's trust. The parent who says one thing and does another is not going to gain a child's trust. Obviously, it is impossible to be consistent 100% of the time. Concentrate on your general track record.

If you want your child to trust you, please behave like the adults in the family. Parents who act like children themselves threaten their child's self-esteem. All children need strong role models. Using drugs, excessive drinking, foul language, excessive anger and inappropriate behavior in front of your children are totally out of the question. Seek professional help if necessary in order to make changes in the family system.

Trust is so fragile. It takes so much time and energy to build, but only seconds to destroy. Lies, ridicule, and disrespect are guaranteed to make a child feel betrayed. Consider the fact that all of your actions serve as a model for your children. I am not suggesting that you always have a smile on your face and sweetness in your voice. Feeling angry and frustrated is part of raising a family, but disrespect and ridicule are not appropriate ways of releasing your anger. In fact, disrespect and ridicule are such strong low self-esteem messages that I would consider this behavior emotionally abusive. Emotional abuse leaves scars just as much as physical abuse. If you find yourself developing these patterns of communication at home, please speak to a mental health professional. Your own personal frustrations coming from somewhere in the family system may be spilling over on other family members.

How Would You Rate Your Listening Skills?

Rate your skills from 1 (needs work) to 5 (very good).

Time	1	2	3	4	5
Eye Contact	1	2	3	4	5
Listening For Feelings	1	2	3	4	5
Interrupting	1	2	3	4	5
Taking Away Feelings	1	2	3	4	5
Distracted	1	2	3	4	5
Reading Nonverbals	1	2	3	4	5

Like any skill, listening takes practice. I suggest you practice the behaviors listed above one at a time. Becoming a good listener is a process that requires time and patience. Mastering this important skill will improve your communication in all aspects of your life.

QUICK REMINDERS

1. Effective listening is one of the most powerful high self-esteem messages that a child can receive.

2. The use of effective attending skills "opens up" communication.

    - Make eye contact

    - Be physically available

    - Avoid distractions

    - Pay attention

3. Avoid common roadblocks to good listening.

    - Interrupting

    - Thinking ahead

    - Taking away feelings

4. Nonverbal behavior (tone of voice, facial expression and body language) accounts for 90% of the meaning of our conversation.

5. Building trust and accepting your child's feelings will set the stage for high self-esteem.

JOURNAL

What have I learned about my children, my family and myself?

5

WHAT DO I SAY NOW ?

> *Every time I tell my mother I hate school, she yells at me and makes me feel like a bad girl.*
>
> *Carol, 7-years-old*

Quite often, we respond without thinking. We react because someone has pushed one of our buttons. While juggling a few balls in the air trying to be all things to all people, who has the time to step back and figure out the best response? Instead, we react with statements like:

- "Are you crazy?"

- "When I was your age . . ."

- "You shouldn't think that way!"

- "How many times have I told you ?"

- "That will never work."

- "That's ridiculous."

Reacting, Not Responding

Reacting gets us into trouble because when we react, we are not listening. Reacting prevents us from reaching a level of communication that creates a feeling of connection or understanding for the child and the parent. Feeling heard builds a child's self-esteem. If a parent's response is on the same page as a child's thoughts and emotions, a connection is felt on both sides. When our message and feelings are acknowledged, self-esteem increases.

Parents As Problem Solvers

Parents often feel responsible for solving every problem a child presents to them. When our children come to us with a situation, we feel the need to provide solutions. Our response style is to provide the answers or feel angry and inadequate because we don't have the answers. All too often, we define the good parent as the one who solves problems and, therefore, doesn't have problems. The bad parent is filled with problems and doesn't have any of the answers. Right? Wrong.

How would you feel if you were to call your mother or father and find yourself in the following conversation?

> YOU: "I just don't know what to do about my job."
>
> PARENT: "What do you mean, you don't know what to do? Of course, you must quit as soon as possible. I know this will make you much happier. You'll find something much better suited for you."
>
> YOU: "But, I'm not sure. . . ."
>
> PARENT: "I'm going to begin looking at some websites tonight. I'll save you some time."
>
> YOU: "I don't know if I'll be any better off if I make a change."
>
> PARENT: "Don't you think I know what's good for you? Why are giving me such a hard time? Why bother talking to me if you're not going to listen? You always were a stubborn kid!"

Chuckling? This is exactly what we do with our children. We rush in with solutions, advice and answers. After all, aren't we more experienced? Don't we have the ability to fix things so we can all move on? Is it any wonder our children appear angry, rejected or feel inadequate when we are trying so hard to help? The spiral of emotions continues as we react to our children's anger and frustration with our own anger and frustration.

Often, the presenting problem or the words that are being spoken are a camouflage or smoke screen for the real underlying issues. It is rare that any of us approach a subject by getting right to the heart of the matter.

Let's go back to our telephone conversation with your parents.

YOU: "I just don't know what to do about my job."

Consider the variety of underlying feelings and conflicts these thoughts may be related to. Consider the entire family system.

1. Are you having a problem with one of the children and feeling that you need more time at home? Is the problem surfacing at school?

2. Is the job interfering with your relationship with your partner?

3. Are you being promoted and feeling anxious about more success and responsibility?

4. Is it time for a raise and your tendency is not to assert yourself?

5. Are you thinking about having another baby?

6. Do you have a new co-worker who is younger and less experienced who is outshining you?

I could go on and on hypothesizing about your true feelings behind the words.

- ### THE REAL ART OF LISTENING IS RESPONDING TO A PERSON'S FEELINGS, NOT HIS/HER WORDS

In order to build self-esteem, we must offer children opportunities to explore their feelings and dilemmas. Through this type of exploration, children establish a sense of personal competence and independence and they learn to make decisions and have opinions. This does not in any way leave you out of the picture. In fact, your role is vital. The following is a wonderful example that shows us why rushing in to solve the problem is not always what a child needs. A six-year-old child who just lost a tooth asked, "Daddy, is there really a tooth fairy?" A simple question, but so many complex issues. Do we burst his bubble? At what age is a child told there is no tooth fairy, Santa Claus, Easter Bunny, etc.? If we lie, are we teaching our children to be deceitful and dishonest?

The following dialogue illustrates what could have been missed if this parent rushed in with solutions, rather than using the opportunity to open up communication. Notice how this parent clarifies his child's feelings.

SON: "Dad, is there really a tooth fairy?"

DAD: "Sounds like you're not sure what to believe."

SON: "Well, if there's a tooth fairy, how does it get in the house?"

DAD: "You're wondering who lets the tooth fairy in?"

SON: "I don't want anyone coming into the house when I'm sleeping."

DAD: "You sound scared."

SON: "I am. Can people get in our house while we're sleeping?"

DAD. "No. I lock the doors very tightly at night."

SON: "So how will the tooth fairy leave me my money?"

DAD: "Maybe he (she) can leave it in the mailbox and I'll take it in the morning."

SON: "I like that idea."

If Dad simply rushed in with a: "Yes, there is a tooth fairy" or "No, there isn't a tooth fairy", he would not have gotten to the real issue here. His son was preoccupied with strangers in his home at night. If you are like many parents, you might have approached this situation hearing only the words rather than the feelings behind the words. This conversation could have easily escalated to a series of low self-esteem messages including:

- "That's a ridiculous question!"

- "Tooth fairies are for babies."

- "You're too old to believe in that nonsense."

- "Be glad you're getting money. Who cares where it comes from?"

- "You're a bad boy. Tooth fairies only visit good boys."

Responding to the feelings behinds the words leads to deeper understanding of this young boy's inner thoughts. The results? The child feels heard and understood, building his self-esteem. The parent feels competent, building his self-esteem.

Giving and Receiving Feedback

Feedback is the information that flows between people. First, your child sends you a message:

- "Hi, Mom!"

- Storming into a room.

- Refusing to go to the bathroom.

- Smiling.

Then, you (the parent) receive the message and send feedback (verbal and nonverbal) to the child. This feedback can be effective or ineffective. Ineffective feedback can be categorized into three main groups:

- Judging

- Sending solutions

- Avoiding the other's concerns

These roadblocks create defensiveness, resistance and resentment in any relationship and certainly diminish self-esteem. Although all of us use some of these ineffective techniques at various times, becoming more aware of your behavior is the first giant step toward change. There are no perfect parents, so concentrate on your willingness to experiment with new behavior.

Many families I work with come in complaining or enraged about their children's misbehavior. As I observe the family interacting, it becomes clear that a new communication style is what is needed to address the problems for everyone. As each member of the family begins to listen and respond appropriately (with less reacting), it is not uncommon for many of the problem behaviors to disappear.

Ice Breakers

If you sense that something is on your child's mind based on his behavior, facial expressions, tone of voice and posture, you may need to break the ice for communication. Picture your child walking into the kitchen for lunch with an unhappy expression on his face. What feedback do you offer?

"What's your problem?"

"Lighten up, buddy."   JUDGEMENTS

"Here we go again."

"Turn on the television. You'll feel better."

"How about reading a story together?"   SOLUTIONS

"Why don't you work on your project today?"

"Nothing could be that bad."   AVOIDING
                                           THE CHILD'S
"What do you have to be in a bad mood   CONCERNS
about?"

Instead of slipping into these roadblocks, perhaps an icebreaker is what is needed. For example:

- ***"Looks like something is bothering you. Would you like to talk about it?"***

Describe the behavior you observe and issue an invitation to talk. Communicate your sincerity with eye contact and appropriate body language. Remember, if your child wants to remain silent, respect his wishes and give him space. Just leave it alone and go about your business. When your child is ready, he will share with you. Nagging and asking dozens of questions will force your child to retreat. This strategy does not facilitate communication.

Minimal Encouragers

Once your child is talking, participate nonverbally. Maintaining eye contact on your child's level helps tremendously. Short responses now and then (known as minimal encouragers) communicate your involvement, without drowning out your child or breaking the mood. Minimal encouragers serve as a high self-esteem message as they say:

- ***"Keep going. I am listening and I understand."***

The following is a list of some commonly used minimal encouragers.

I see.	Sure.
Right.	So?
Yes.	For instance?
Really?	Then?
And?	Uh-huh.
Go on.	Repeating 1-2 words.

Practice this with a friend or partner. See how much of your part of the conversation you can carry on using minimal encouragers. You will be very surprised at the outcome. Chances are you will hear most of what is being said with a greater understanding of the message. The conversation will flow and you will be helping the other person to express his true feelings. This is a skill that must be developed, so continue to practice.

Openers And Closers

You have a choice with each new interaction with your child. You can open the door to fuller, richer, expanded understandings or you can close the door abruptly. Many circumstances lead to closed responses in the family system like stress, fatigue, defensiveness and losing your patience, just to name a few. The following are some classic examples of closed responses:

- "I've heard enough of you!"

- "Don't talk to me like that."

- "End of discussion."

- "Who ever told you you're entitled to an opinion?"

- "Grow up."

- "Stop complaining."

All of the above closed responses are guaranteed to squelch a child's self-esteem. Closed responses block communication by showing no understanding of your child's feelings and often go hand in hand with negative nonverbal behaviors like frowns, angry hand gestures and a disgusted tone of voice.

Open responses show that you understand what your child is saying (verbally and nonverbally) and are a golden opportunity to enhance a child's self-esteem. Open responses send the following high self-esteem messages:

- "I am opening the door for more communication."

- "I would like to understand you."

- "I will help you sort out your feelings."

Questions can be open and closed as well. Closed questions are answered with a short, specific response like "yes" or "no". Open questions, on the other hand, are an invitation for your child to explore his thoughts and feelings. Open questions provide an opportunity to express feelings and thoughts on a blank canvas. A good talk show host is usually quite expert at the use of open questions. Watching your favorite talk show will help you to get the hang of open questioning. Concentrate on beginning your questions with how, what and could. Stay away from why, because why questions tend to put people on the spot. Here are several examples:

- "How do you spend your time with your friends?"

- "What are some of the things that trouble you with your friends?"

- "Could you tell me more about how the fights start?"

Practice with a friend, partner, co-worker or one of the children. Notice how you are facilitating the conversation with the use of open questions. Building your child's self-esteem requires you to be in the role of facilitator, rather than the role of judge, problem solver or feeling denier. I cannot overemphasize enough the importance of facilitating communication between you and your child. I guarantee you that the more you experience your role as a parent facilitator, the more enthusiastically you will seize every opportunity your child brings you for opening up communication and building self-esteem. Family situations, which historically have escalated into screaming matches, will now take a different turn. In order to make this happen, you must not focus on agreeing or disagreeing with your child. You are not there to judge. Our children certainly know how to push our buttons, but remember that reacting is not responding. Instead, picture yourself as a mirror for your child's thoughts and feelings. We call this reflective listening. Concentrate on the feelings behind the words and the feelings behind the behaviors. A parent's reflective response demonstrates understanding and acceptance, the cornerstones of self-esteem. If a child is talking about a problem, the reflection of feelings helps him understand his own emotions and move toward solving the problem. This response on our part:

1. Initially removes us from judging

2. Frees us from our role as problem-solver and fixer

Here are four steps to help you begin your practice of reflective listening:

1. Listen for the feelings behind the words and observe the feelings behind the behaviors.

2. Make a mental note of the content of the message.

3. Observe body language.

4. Put yourself in the child's shoes. Ask yourself: "If I were you, what would I be feeling?"

Let's apply these four steps to the following situation. Your child wakes up this morning and is beginning to complain of a headache and a stomachache. Just as you're considering what you'll do if he needs to stay home today, he says: "I don't want to be in the school play. I can't memorize those lines." Your daughter had a leading role in the school play last year and your son was recently chosen for a part in his class play.

Some typical closed responses to this situation include:

- "Your sister never had this problem." (Judgment)

- "You're smart. You can do it." (Judgment)

- "You're always complaining!" (Judgment)

- "Hurry up and get ready for school." (Denial)

- "You'll do fine." (Denial)

- "We'll work on this morning, noon and night if we have to." (Fixer)

- "I'll call your teacher and discuss taking you out of the play." (Fixer)

Let's switch gears and practice using open reflective responses. We will begin by referring to our four-step process.

1. **What are his feelings based on his words and his behavior?**
   Discouraged, scared, uneasy, frustrated, worried.

2. **What is the content of his message?**
   Doesn't want to be in play. Can't memorize lines.

3. **Body language?**
   Sluggish, face distorted, dragging, slow speech, low pitch.

4. **How would I feel?**
   Scared to fail.
   Worried I wouldn't be as good as my sister.
   Concerned that the other kids will laugh at me.
   Concerned that my parents will feel disappointed.

Using open reflective responses, you might say:

- "Sounds like you're feeling scared because you don't want to fail."

- "Maybe you're discouraged because it seems so difficult to remember your lines."

- "You're worried because you really want to do a nice job."

- "You seem frustrated because memorizing lines and getting up in front of an audience is such a big responsibility."

However you choose to respond (and there is no right or wrong way), a reflective response will open up communication and serve to let your child know that you understand and accept his feelings.

Reflective Responses

How do you form a reflective response? A simple format for reflective listening is:

You feel_____because_____
_____

Sounds like you feel_____because_____
_____

Maybe you feel_____because_____
_____

It appears you feel_____because _____
_____

You're feeling _____because _____
_____

I get the impression you feel_____because _____
_____

I guess you're feeling_____because_____
_____

Initially, many parents object to this pattern for responding to their children. They feel it is fake, contrived or lacking in spontaneity. I acknowledge these reservations. Give this a chance, though, and see what results you come up with. Many parents I work with complain at first, but then find reflective listening extremely successful for dealing with problem situations. Rather than yelling, ignoring or giving a "that's nice" response, parents find that responding reflectively leads to more meaningful exchanges and a closer feeling of connectedness with their children. The children respond with increased communication, less conflict, more cooperation and heightened self-esteem. Who can argue with these results?

Feelings

To be an effective listener, you need a variety of feeling words at your fingertips. You can pull from this list for your reflective responses, or if your child's behavior is baffling you, refer to this list and ask yourself, "What is my child feeling?"

Isn't it incredible when you stop to consider the range of feelings you and your child may experience?

accepting	calm	defensive
aggressive	carefree	demanding
ambitious	caring	dependable
angry	cautious	depressed
annoyed	cheerful	determined
anxious	clever	disappointed
assertive	confident	embarrassed
aware	confused	energetic
bitter	cooperative	enthusiastic
bold	courageous	excited
bored	cranky	exhausted
brave	critical	fearful

foolish	lazy	precise
friendly	lively	pretentious
gentle	lonely	protective
giving	loving	proud
grateful	malicious	quarrelsome
greedy	materialistic	quiet
guilty	mature	radical
happy	merry	realistic
helpful	modest	reasonable
helpless	naïve	rebellious
honorable	negative	reflective
hostile	nervous	regretful
hurt	normal	rejected
imaginative	oblivious	relaxed
immature	observant	reliable
impressionable	organized	resentful
inconsiderate	original	reserved
independent	overconfident	respectful
ingenious	overemotional	responsive
insensitive	overprotective	rigid
insincere	overwhelmed	sad
intelligent	passive	sarcastic
intuitive	patient	satisfied
irresponsible	perceptive	selfish
irritable	persuasive	sensitive
jealous	petty	shy
jovial	playful	silly
juvenile	pleased	skillful
kind	pompous	sociable
knowledgeable	powerful	spontaneous

stable	tired	unreasonable
strong	tough	useful
stubborn	trusting	vain
surprised	trustworthy	vulnerable
sympathetic	unassuming	warm
temperamental	unaware	wise
tender	uncertain	wishful
tense	uncomfortable	withdrawn
thoughtful	unpredictable	worried

"I" Messages

Blame is at the core of low self-esteem. "You" messages attack and blame your child. For example:

- "Where have you been? You are so inconsiderate!"

- "You never put your bike away. You are so irresponsible."

"I" messages are a way of describing your feelings by focusing on your child's behavior without attacking and blaming. To form an "I" message, describe the behavior, describe how you feel and state why you feel that way. For example:

- "When you are late, I feel upset because I have no idea where you are."

- "When you don't put your bike away, I feel angry because I have to get out of the car and move it."

Practice sending "I" messages to your children and see how it feels. "I" messages give you the opportunity to express yourself effectively in a way that can be heard by others.

Positive Feelings Count

Our tendency is to use our newly acquired skills to help us only when there is a problem. Please continue to do so, but don't forget the joyful moments of the day when reflective listening will let your child know that you are fully present. Often, if no one is crying, screaming, whining or bleeding, we do not listen to what is going on around us. I encourage you to use reflective listening as a means of sharing a happy moment with your child. Reflective listening is also an excellent means of reinforcing improvements in behavior.

There are many instances when a big smile, an approving glance, a tender touch, a warm hug, or a playful pat on the back means more to your child than any words could possibly express. A nonverbal response can get right to the heart of the matter since we experience nonverbal messages at a considerably deeper level than verbal messages.

Follow Your Instincts

Paying more attention to experts, books and others, rather than following our own instincts, is a common habit for all of us. If you feel anxious about making decisions related to your children, these feelings will be communicated to your children, resulting in them feeling nervous and insecure. Their self-esteem will definitely suffer. The messages you may be sending include:

- "I don't know what to do."

- "I'm afraid to make a decision."

- "Someone else understands my child more than I do."

- "I don't feel competent enough to know what would be best."

- Nonverbal messages that communicate all of the above.

The child is left feeling anxious, needing a strong authority figure to "take charge" of the situation. Feeling comfortable in your position as CEO of the family will help your children to feel safe and secure, adding to their self-esteem.

The following is a situation which illustrates a parent who has overruled the experts. A parent of a thirteen-year-old boy described the difficulties his son was having in seventh grade. The boy was on the intellectual side and had no friends. As the situation grew worse, the boy appeared terribly depressed at home and even began to talk about killing himself. The father went to the school and met with the principal. The school felt that this was a phase and certainly no cause for alarm. The father was not at all satisfied with what he heard. His inner voice continued to repeat, "There is a problem here." On the other hand, the principal had many years of experience with children this age, so the father tried to talk himself out of his worrying. Unfortunately, the next year brought no change so, with the father's insistence, the child was seen by the school social worker. Here, again, the school social worker did not feel the boy needed a great deal of attention. At this point, the father's heart was breaking for his son, so he decided to take him to see a psychologist in the community. Once again, the psychologist did not see the need for treatment. Finally, one year later, the father met another parent at a seminar who recommended a psychologist in the community who specializes in the treatment of gifted children. After several months of weekly visits, the father said there was a world of difference. His son loved his weekly sessions with the therapist and has made many strides socially. The psychologist recommended a summer camp for intellectually gifted children. At the camp, the boy found his niche and developed friendships that sustain him during the school year. He is in high school now and progressing beautifully. With all of the conflicting messages this father received, his instincts led him in the right direction for his son.

Following your instincts provides many important strong high self-esteem messages for your child:

- "I hear you."

- "I understand you."

- "I won't be sidetracked by others."

- "I have confidence in my ability to make decisions about you."

While I certainly value the opinions of teachers, administrators, psychologists and physicians, ultimately, a parent often knows his child best. If your instincts are telling you there is a problem, don't back down. Parents, you are the real experts when it comes to your children!

QUICK REMINDERS

1. Parents are facilitators.

2. Respond, don't react.

3. The real art of listening is responding to a person's feelings, not his or her words.

4. DO:
   Do break the ice.
   Do use minimal encouragers.
   Do use open statements and open questions.
   Do listen reflectively.

5. DON'T:
   Do not stand in judgment.
   Do not fix all problems.
   Do not avoid and deny the feelings of others.
   Do not use closed statements and closed questions.

6. Follow your instincts!

JOURNAL

What have I learned about my children, my family and myself?

6

ALL FAMILIES DEAL WITH CONFLICT

> *Our home is a battlefield. I would love to get through one day without the screaming and bickering. It begins in the morning getting the kids ready for school, and continues through dinner, homework and bedtime. My wife and I are barely able to have a civil conversation without attacking each other. I am seriously considering running away from home.*
>
> *Tom, 35-years-old*

Conflicts in a family are inevitable. Whether you are dealing with a child who doesn't want to nap, a teenager who doesn't want a curfew or an adult child who doesn't want to hear your opinion, learning the skills to manage conflict effectively will be a tremendous help to you.

Does Conflict Serve A Purpose?

So many people detest conflict, yet conflict serves so many purposes. Conflict helps us to become aware of problems that need to be solved. There are many times when a situation needs changing and old habits need readjusting. Conflict helps to reduce the day-to-day annoyances of relating to someone. Conflict deepens a relationship. If the message that underlies each conflict is, "No matter what, I love you," the emotional bonds in your family will grow stronger.

Conflicts We All Face

Even before the birth of your child, you may have dealt with conflict as a result of decisions needing to be made and various people offering advice. As you moved from partners to parents, your roles changed dramatically, opening up many new areas for conflict. Each stage of raising a child presents a new set of challenges as well as a new set of potential conflicts.

The following are examples of common conflicts that cover the period from infancy through the elementary school years:

- Should we breastfeed or bottle-feed?

- Will we accept help from family and friends?

- Should I return to work?

- What type of childcare works for us?

- How do we share the responsibilities?

- Is my partner involved enough?

- How do we discipline our child?

- How do we handle temper tantrums?

- How do we choose a school?

- How do we manage the daily schedules?

- How do we accomplish homework without a battle?

- How do we engage our children's cooperation in daily chores?

- How do I fit in any free time for myself?

- How much time is important for us as a couple away from the children?

Adolescence presents a unique set of challenges as your children are increasingly exposed to outside pressures at a time when they are trying so hard to fit in. At the same time, you need to offer them more freedom (in small steps) so they will be prepared to leave home at an appropriate age and manage their own lives. Teenagers want to be in charge of their own lives and resent just about any interference from their parents. With parents still in charge, the family becomes extremely fertile ground for conflict.

Letting go when your children become young adults is very difficult. Conflict continues as we are faced with renegotiating our roles. After all, don't you still have conflicts with your parents?

I do not want to give the impression that raising a child is one conflict after another, but I do want to present a realistic view. Although a family can offer you much joy and satisfaction, when two or more people live together, conflict is inevitable. The purpose of this chapter is to become comfortable with conflict and learn to approach every conflict as a problem that can be solved. Managing conflict effectively is a skill we need everyday as we interact with all members of our family system. Keep in mind, you are always modeling behavior for your children who are watching and learning from you all of the time. Mastering the important skill of managing conflict will lead to stronger relationships and help to build your child's self-esteem.

Using The "Same Wrong Solution"

How many times have we dealt with a conflict using a method or solution which just doesn't work, only to find ourselves using more of the same wrong solution the next time around? Most of us do this, but can't understand why we are getting no results. Consider the parent who asks a toddler over and over again not to bang her toy on the table. The more the parent observes the behavior, the more frustrated and angry the parent becomes. Instead, try a new solution by removing the toy and engaging the toddler in a new activity. Although this sounds so simple, we don't realize how often we continue to use the same strategy to resolve a problem over and over again, even though we never get any results.

When conflict strikes, we all get stuck in many familiar traps. As our frustration builds, high self-esteem messages dwindle and are replaced with low self-esteem messages:

- "Don't you get the message?"

- "What's wrong with you?"

- "Are you hard of hearing?"

- "What's your problem?"

- "I'm sick of you!"

- "No wonder you don't have any friends!"

- "You'll never amount to anything!"

Are there any other low self-esteem messages you can add to this list?

_____

_____

_____

_____

Looking Back

There are many factors that influence how we react to a conflict. How our families dealt with conflict when we grew up has a major impact on our response to conflict today.

How did your family deal with conflict when you were growing up?

_____

_____

_____

_____

How would you describe your reaction to conflict today?

_____

_____

_____

_____

Do you see any connections?

_____

_____

_____

_____

Managing A Conflict

What is the goal of the conflict?

- **Achieving your personal goals:** You are in conflict because you have a goal that conflicts with another person's goal. For instance, I don't want my child to have ice cream now because it will ruin her appetite before dinner.

- **Maintaining the relationship(s):** You are in conflict because you may not want to upset the relationship(s). For instance, I often feel like my child hates me, so I am walking on eggshells.

Given these two concerns (personal goals and relationship goals), there are five styles of managing conflict. Each of these styles has its place and it is useful to feel comfortable with a variety of styles.

1. **Withdrawal** - You avoid conflict, even if it means giving up your personal goals and being uninvolved in the relationship. You believe it is hopeless to resolve the conflict.

2. **Force** - You overpower your opponents by forcing them to accept your solution to the conflict. Your goals are all that count. You aren't concerned with the needs of others. You feel it's a matter of winning or losing, and, of course, you want to be the winner. If people don't like you, that's their problem.

3. **Smoothing Over** - You like to keep everything in the relationship smooth, even if it means giving up your own goals. Conflicts should be avoided because they only cause trouble. I'll let you have what you want, so that you'll like me.

4. **Compromising** - You seek a solution to a conflict where both sides gain something. You are willing to sacrifice part of your goals and make changes in the relationship in order to find agreement for the common good.

5. **Confronting** - You see conflicts as problems to be solved and seek solutions that satisfy everyone involved. You believe conflicts reduce tension and are an opportunity to air negative feelings. You're not satisfied until a solution is found.

How would you identify your conflict management style?

_____

_____

_____

_____

Exercise: List two major conflicts you have had with a child in the family and describe how you handled the conflict. Identify your conflict management style in each example.

1. Conflict:

_____

_____

_____

_____

How I handled the conflict:

_____

_____

_____

_____

My conflict management style(s):

_____

_____

_____

_____

How else could I have handled the conflict?

_____

_____

_____

_____

2. Conflict:

_____

_____

_____

_____

How I handled the conflict:

_____

_____

_____

_____

My conflict management style(s):

_____

_____

_____

_____

How else could I have handled the conflict?

_____

_____

_____

_____

Conflict Resolution

Since we all face conflicts with our children, it is worthwhile to prepare ourselves in advance with a set of rules that will help us to avoid the conflict disintegrating into escalating low self-esteem messages.

1. Make sure you treat your child with respect. Avoid low self-esteem messages like:

    - "What a stupid idea."

    - "That's the most ridiculous thing I ever heard."

    - Body language that says, "You're out of your mind."

2. Listen until you fully experience the other side. Concentrate on accurately reflecting feelings. Do not offer explanations and apologies. Just LISTEN!

3. State your views, needs and feelings. Be brief. Say what you mean and mean what you say. Disclose your feelings.

4. Place the emphasis on: "We have a problem." Your focus then becomes a collaborative search for solution.

5. Never attempt to resolve a conflict when one or both of you is emotionally upset. Allow for a cooling off period.

6. Involve your child in suggesting solutions to the conflict. Do not evaluate any of the suggestions.

Avoiding Conflict

Although we all face conflict, there are ways to eliminate certain unnecessary conflicts. Children thrive best when there is order and regularity. They are happier when they know what to expect. Consistent routines will reduce conflict. Do you have daily routines for:

- Waking up?

- Meals?

- Bedtime and curfews?

Describe your daily routine:

_____

_____

_____

_____

Do you have family rules? You will be more effective if you set a few reasonable rules. Children will be able to remember them and you will be able to enforce them.

What are your family rules?

_____

_____

_____

_____

Avoiding Conflict

Finally, avoid conflict by picking your battles. If everything is an issue for you, you will experience constant conflict. Examine your priorities. Learn to look away and walk away when it is appropriate. If this is impossible for you, you probably need help managing your anger, stress and your need to maintain control.

Conflict and Expectations

Are your expectations realistic? If your expectations are unrealistic and you are constantly expecting more and more from your child, you will always feel disappointed and your child will feel disappointed in herself and angry at you. Your child will feel that she can never measure up, and her self-esteem will suffer. Perhaps, the problem lives inside of you, and you are expecting too much from yourself. Until you get a handle on this, it will be difficult for you to be fair with your children. Having realistic expectations that your child can fulfill will give her a feeling of success and competence. On the other hand, parents who expect too little may be contributing to a child's feelings that she is incapable and incompetent. This is often a fine line to walk, so we need to re-evaluate our expectations often.

Exercise:

1. What conflicts did you observe in the family this week?

_____

_____

_____

_____

2. What conflict management styles did you observe?

_____

_____

_____

_____

Conflict is part of any close relationship. Reflect on how you approached each conflict situation and consider experimenting with new strategies. Relationships grow stronger when conflicts are managed well.

QUICK REMINDERS

1. Conflicts between parents and children are inevitable. It is the way we choose to respond to a conflict that determines the effect the conflict will have on our child's self-esteem.

2. DO:
   Do listen!
   Do use reflective listening.
   Do stick to the issue.

3. DON'T:
   Don't be disrespectful.
   Don't list other offenses.
   Don't use the "same wrong solution" over and over again.

4. Work on feeling comfortable with a variety of conflict management styles:
   Withdrawal   Compromising
   Force   Confronting
   Smoothing Over

5. When resolving a conflict:
   Treat your child with respect.
   Listen until you experience the other side.
   State your views, needs and feelings.
   Search for a solution.
   Evaluate.

JOURNAL

What have I learned about my children, my family and myself?

7

HOW ANGER AND STRESS AFFECT SELF-ESTEEM

> *The stress is unbelievable. I find myself running in so many directions at once, yet I feel I just can't seem to catch up. My fuse has become so short and I blow up easily. At this point, I feel angry at everyone and everything. I know I have legitimate gripes, but often I feel guilty after I lose my temper. When I keep these feelings in, I end up feeling depressed. I know the kids are affected by all of this, but I don't know what to change.*
>
> ***Working mother, 2 children***

Sound familiar? I don't know a family that doesn't have to deal with anger and stress. Coping effectively with these feelings will greatly enhance your child's self-esteem. Not coping well with these feelings will lead to an increasing number of low self-esteem messages, damaging your child's self-esteem.

Anger is an emotion that occurs regularly in every person. So many of us are afraid to feel our anger or feel uncomfortable around someone who is angry. Anger occurs when we are not getting something we want or would like and serves a number of different functions including:

1. Anger allows you to express feelings and thoughts which might not have been expressed if you were not angry.

2. Anger can be a signal that an event or a behavior that is frustrating or annoying is taking place.

95

3.   Anger may lead to problem solving, strengthening the relationship.

4.   Anger can overcome anxiety and fear and lead to taking action.

5.   Anger is a sign that something is going on that needs to be changed.

6.   Anger can also have many positive effects and strengthen emotional bonds.

Managing Your Own Anger

Everyone gets angry. Anger is often a reaction to frustration, hurt or fear. If anger is expressed in a destructive manner, anger can do a great deal of damage to a child's self-esteem. The following are examples of statements that express anger in a destructive fashion:

- "Don't talk to me."

- "I'm sick of you."

- "Leave me alone."

- "Get lost."

- "You're a real pain."

- "You're nothing but a spoiled brat."

Is anger a problem for you? If you have periodic outbursts, it is. If your child has periodic outbursts, it is. If you never feel angry, you may have a significant problem. The anger may come out in other ways, including physical symptoms such as ulcers and high blood pressure. Maybe you never feel angry, but you're often depressed. Depression is anger turned inward. There are also those whose anger is expressed indirectly toward others with sarcastic remarks, dirty looks or putdowns.

Angry outbursts have their consequences. As a parent, you may find yourself feeling quite guilty, after the fact. You can't take back what has already been said and your child may feel extremely anxious after hearing your words. The outburster often has no idea what he stated in a fit of rage. When you feel angry, it is so important to choose your words carefully. At times, our outbursts of anger get us what we want for the moment. A nagging child stops nagging. A crying child runs to his room. In the long run, though, we are doing more harm than good. As a parent, you are entitled to your angry feelings. The key issue is the way you express those feelings.

Exercise:

Complete the following sentences:

1. I feel angry when my children _____

_____

2. When I'm angry at my children, I usually _____

_____

_____

3. After expressing my anger, I feel _____

4. The way I express anger usually makes my children

_____

_____

5. What are some of your children's typical behaviors or behavior patterns that make you feel angry?

_____

_____

_____

_____

6. *How do you respond to these situations?*

_____

_____

_____

_____

7. *What are some alternative ways to deal with these situations?*

_____

_____

_____

_____

Guidelines For Expressing Your Anger

DO's

1. Do - Make the expression a release of pent-up emotions. Anger needs to be expressed in a way that gets it over and done with. Anger is NOT a feeling to hold on to.

2. Do - Express your anger to the APPROPRIATE person and make it to the point. "I feel angry when ....."

3. Do - Stay focused on this ONE particular situation.

4. Do - Give your child a chance to respond after you've expressed your anger.

5. Do - Express positive feelings (high self-esteem messages) as well as your anger.

DON'Ts

1. Don't - Attempt to prove you were right or that you are morally superior. Try to solve the problem and manage the situation constructively.

2. Don't - Rehash other unrelated or related incidents.

3. Don't - Be sarcastic.

4. Don't - Resort to name-calling.

5. Don't - Make alot of accusations.

6. Don't - Physically attack your child.

Rules For Managing Anger Constructively

In order to manage your anger constructively, the following set of rules can be very helpful.

1. Recognize and acknowledge the fact that you are angry. Anger is a natural, healthy human feeling.

2. Decide whether or not you wish to express your anger. Hostility will build up if you sweep your anger under the rug for days or weeks. On the other hand, there are times when avoidance may be the most effective action to take.

3. It is important to have ways of responding to provocations other than getting angry or feeling depressed. One alternative is relaxation. Learn to relax through meditation, yoga, exercise, listening to music or taking quiet time when your anger has been triggered. Go into another room and count slowly to ten if you have to.

4. Express your anger directly and effectively when it is appropriate to do so. Expressing anger can clear the air so that positive feelings can once again be felt and expressed.

Dealing With An Angry Child

We can compare an angry child to a dam ready to burst. A precipitating incident, plus readiness on the part of the angry child, precedes an outburst of anger. Anger is generally building as a result of frustration, not feeling good about oneself, an immature way of asserting oneself, a defensive maneuver to keep others away or a desperate way of reaching out.

How do you usually respond to your child when he is angry?

_____

_____

_____

_____

- Know and understand your response to anger.

- An angry attack comes from an unhappy person. His unhappiness is probably unrelated to the precipitating incident.

- Let the angry person talk and get out his emotions.

- Accept the child's right to be angry.

- Use your nonverbal skills to show you are listening.

- When your child is ready, respond to his feeling using reflective listening to communicate your concern.

When there is an explosion, there is not too much you can say or do until the outburst is over. Your child will not be able to hear you until he releases most of the angry feelings. One of the more difficult challenges in responding to an angry child is being able to live through the intense emotions without becoming angry and having an outburst yourself.

Exercise:

PARENT: "What football game? (What birthday party?) Everytime I need your help, you're watching TV or on the phone. I am tired of all your excuses. If you can't do your chores around the house, you'd better plan to stay home Saturday afternoon."

CHILD: "You're always picking on me. You never let me do anything that's fun! I hate you!"

How does it feel when your child is this angry with you? How do you respond?

_____

_____

_____

_____

There are times when your child's anger at you may be displaced anger. You will probably have to live through a few outbursts before your child is ready to talk. Use reflective listening and investigate other areas of the family system. Ask yourself if your child is reacting to any changes in your own life. The chart below may help you identify the root of your child's anger.

<u>Family</u>	<u>School</u>	<u>Work</u>
Divorce	Peer pressure	Parent over involvement
Remarriage	Rejection by peers	Added stress on parent
Marital Tension	Teacher too stressed	Work too difficult on parent
Any change	Any change	Any change

Is your anger at your child displaced anger coming from a different part of the family system? You may be angry at someone else in the family system and displacing your anger on your child. Feelings need to be expressed, but there may be times when you are not able to express your anger directly at the person provoking you (like your boss or mother-in-law). Take some time to examine your own thoughts and feelings if you are going through a rough patch. Find someone to talk to and/or write your thoughts in a journal.

Anger is tough. Feel good about your ability to manage your anger successfully. Congratulate yourself for a job well done. Don't expect perfection. Everyone blows up from time to time and regrets something they said or did. Remember, there are no perfect parents.

Consequences

If you are angry because your child is not cooperating or misbehaving, yelling and nagging will not help to create any changes. When you are yelling and nagging, you feel out of control, helpless and ineffective. If you want to correct or modify a child's behavior, the only intervention that will achieve long lasting results is the use of consequences. It is important to intervene in a situation before you lose your temper. Give your child a warning that there will be a consequence if he does not behave in a specific way. State this warning before you lose control and begin screaming. State the warning when you are feeling a 3-4 on the anger scale of 1-10. Describe the behavior you expect clearly and calmly. For example:

- Describe the behavior: "I expect you to share your toys with your sister."

- Warning: "If you cannot share, I will put these toys away."

- Describe the behavior: " Hitting your brother is not acceptable behavior."

- Warning: "If you continue to hit your brother, you will not go to soccer practice today."

If the misbehavior continues, let your child know that he has made a choice and has chosen the consequence. You should do this before you exceed a 5-6 on the anger scale. If you wait too long, you may lose your temper. Make sure you express only one warning. If there are a series of warnings, then your child knows you don't mean business.

- Consequence: "You made your choice. The toys are being put away since you were not able to share with your sister."

- Consequence: "You made your choice. You will not be going to soccer practice today."

Consequences need to be reasonable and enforceable. When you give your child a consequence, he may begin to whine, cry or ignore you. Your child may attempt to talk you out of the consequence or he may attempt to negotiate with you. If your child tells you he doesn't care about the consequence, do not react. Believe me, he cares! You must not back down. State that there will be many opportunities to cooperate in the future. You have done your job as a parent and can now walk away from the situation. Using consequences now and then will not modify your child's behavior. As a parent, it is imperative that you continue to teach and shape your child's behavior on an ongoing, consistent basis. Consequences are a reality of life for all of us.

Managing Stress

Managing stress is an absolute necessity for building your child's self-esteem. If you are running on an empty tank, you will have nothing to give your children. Everything you have learned thus far won't add up to anything meaningful if you are always on overload.

Long-term stress can have a devastating effect on us. When there never seems to be a break in the stress of daily living, we could be headed for some big problems. A parent who feels overwhelmed will find it difficult to practice the concepts presented in this book far. Genuinely experiencing a feeling of enjoyment in being with your child is vital in order to communicate a feeling of love to your child. How can a parent who is exhausted, pressured, rushed and harried enjoy anything?

What are some typical responses to stress?

Physical Responses:

- A life of rushing
- Feeling withdrawn or depressed
- Increase in smoking or drinking
- Sex life going downhill
- Headaches
- Fluctuation in weight
- Change in sleep habits
- Shortness of breath
- Bursting into tears easily
- Excessive nervous energy
- Speech problems
- Nervous laughter
- Excessive perspiration
- Frequent need to urinate
- Illness such as high blood and ulcers
- Difficulty concentrating
- Frequent heartburn

Emotional Responses:

- Boredom

- Lack of concentration

- Anxiety

- Irritable with family and co-workers

- Difficulty smiling or laughing

- Feeling like an unsuccessful parent

- Feeling alone

- Constant feeling of anger under the surface

- Fear of disease

- Excessive crying

Although most of us experience some of these symptoms from time to time, we must examine the intensity and the duration of the symptomatic behaviors. We might ask ourselves, "How are these symptoms interfering with my functioning in the family and/or at work?" Stress affects our bodies as well as the way we think and feel. The stress each of us experiences during the day ripples throughout the family system and affects all of our relationships in the family.

Exercise:

What creates stress for you in the family?

_____

_____

_____

_____

What do you and/or your partner find stressful at work?

_____

_____

_____

If you are a single-parent, what are the added stressors in your life?

_____

_____

_____

What is stressful for each of your children?

_____

_____

_____

What do you find stressful within your community?

_____

_____

_____

What do you find stressful about living and raising children in our culture?

_____

_____

_____

You probably need a plan for change. Remember, a small change can go a long way and will ripple throughout the entire family system.

What can you do during the course of your week to relieve some of your stress?

_____

_____

_____

_____

My Support System

A big mistake many parents make is believing that they must accomplish everything without any outside help. That's ridiculous! We all need help and support, particularly with the non-stop demands of raising children. Where is help available? It is important to weave a network of supportive people around you. Again, let's look at the family system.

When it comes to the family, we all need someone to talk to. Just as it is important for our children to be listened to, it is equally important for us to have someone who will listen.

List people you can rely on to help you with the children (friends, relatives, caregivers).

_____

_____

_____

_____

List any other resources you use to help you with the daily routines at home.

_____

_____

_____

_____

If you are working, you will benefit from having at least one person who you can talk to about work related issues. Who do you talk to?

_____

_____

_____

_____

Who can you rely on to help with the daily school and after school routines?

_____

_____

_____

_____

What if you child gets sick and you are not available? What if you are delayed at the end of the day? Who can offer you support?

_____

_____

_____

_____

We all need a break from it all. Who can you spend time with for an evening or afternoon out?

_____

_____

_____

_____

Some of us have special interests or hobbies. Who can you share these interests with?

_____

_____

_____

_____

This inventory should help you to see where the gaps are in your support system and help you to plan to reach out for additional support in your life. In which aspect(s) of your life do you think you would benefit from additional support?

_____

Taking Care Of Yourself Influences Self-Esteem

Everyone needs what I call "special treats". We give our children special treats by playing with them, buying them something special or taking them somewhere special. What have you done for yourself lately? Make it your business, particularly when you're beginning to run on empty, to give yourself a treat. It might be a quiet walk, listening to music, a bubble bath or buying yourself a book.

When was the last time you gave yourself a "special treat"?

_____

What do you consider to be special ? _____

_____

When was the last time you spent time alone? _____

_____

_____

Many parents I speak with tell me their only time alone is a few minutes in the bathroom. That is, if they can keep the children out. Everyone needs a few moments of alone time to stare into space in order to decompress, debrief and chill out.

When can you find a few minutes each day to be alone?

_____

_____

_____

_____

When you are angry or stressed, sending high self-esteem messages to your children seems like an impossible task. Before we know what has happened to us, our homes become filled with low self-esteem messages. When children are bombarded with low self-esteem messages from all sides, they are bound to develop problems. By managing your anger and controlling your stress (build and use your support system), it is more likely that you will be able to continue to send high self-esteem messages to everyone in the family.

Seeking Professional Help

If you find yourself struggling with a situation, don't struggle alone. You may be caught in the web of using the same wrong solution over and over again. A fresh perspective from someone outside of the family system might be exactly what you need. Many people are reluctant to reach out for professional help. They want to go it alone or try to convince themselves that their problem isn't big enough. Nonsense. All families experience problems, conflict, anger and stress. Reach out for help before the situation becomes out of control. Self-esteem is a dynamic, ever-changing process, so outside help may be just what you need to turn the situation around.

Exercise:

1. Describe how you expressed your anger in the family this week.

_____

_____

_____

_____

2. Describe how others expressed anger in the family.

_____

_____

_____

_____

3. What people in your support system did you have contact with this week?

_____

_____

_____

_____

4. What did you do for yourself this week?

_____

_____

_____

_____

QUICK REMINDERS

ANGER

1. DO:
   Do express your anger to the appropriate person and make it to the point.
   Do express positive feelings, even though you are angry.

2 DON'T:
   Don't attempt to prove you were right.
   Don't rehash other incidents.
   Don't be sarcastic.
   Don't name call.
   Don't physically attack your child.

STRESS

1. DO:
   Do identify the stresses in your life.
   Do use your support systems.
   Do give yourself special treats.
   Do find a few minutes each day to be alone.

2. DON'T:
   Don't try to be super human.

JOURNAL

What have I learned about my children, my family and myself?

CONCLUSION

I certainly hope that my words have been helpful and that you are able to incorporate the ideas presented in this book into your daily life with your family. As I reflect on these ideas, I find myself observing and evaluating my own behavior in my family and in the world. Do I practice what I preach? "There are no perfect parents" has certainly become a popular slogan of mine. This offers the comfort and reassurance that is needed when life is not going the way we would like it to. More importantly, it is through our own self-acceptance that we can fully accept our children for who they are.

I have become highly sensitized to the high and low self-esteem messages we communicate to each other verbally and nonverbally. As each day ends, our children are left to reflect on a tapestry of high and low self-esteem messages they have experienced throughout the day. The impact we make on these messages is tremendous. Maintaining an awareness of our behavior is a large part of the process of building a child's self-esteem. If we can rise above the day-to-day conflicts and continue to reinforce to our children, "No matter what, I love you," our children will feel safe and secure. We all need to know that we are cherished for our specialness despite the fact that everything is NOT perfect.

When too many low self-esteem messages hit a child from all sides (family, school, friends), a problem is likely to develop. Whether it is a learning, emotional or behavior problem, parents are in the powerful position of helping their children maintain their self-respect and self-esteem throughout the process of change. Remember, self-esteem is dynamic and always changing.

Taking the time to really listen is so important to our children. When someone listens to us, we feel valued. Of course, there are times when we just have too much on our minds to be emotionally available to our children. We need to create time for listening and practice listening. Practice with your children, your friends, fellow workers, and other family members. Ask yourself, "Did I really hear what was being said?" When you truly hear what someone is communicating to you (the feelings behind the words), responding in a way that makes a person feel understood will come more naturally. Reflective listening is a very potent skill for communicating understanding. Feeling understood is a valuable gift that all of us crave. Feeling understood leads to a sense of connectedness and strengthens emotional bonds.

There are no close relationships without conflict. Although many of us cringe at the thought of conflict, it is worthwhile to remember that conflict serves a purpose in our lives. It is often through conflict that a much needed change will finally come about or tensions will be aired that will allow us to go onto new business. The key issue is how we communicate in a conflict situation. It is important to choose your words carefully. Regardless of the size and intensity of the conflict, it is vital to let your child know that he/she is still very much cared about. Sometimes we loose perspective and the memories of more joyful moments tend to slip from our minds. During times of conflict, I frequently look through old photograph albums in order to experience strong positive feelings for my children.

My final thoughts relate to the way we feel when we have nothing left to give. It is important to keep ourselves nourished emotionally so we can nourish our children. Reach out to others for help and support. No one should have to go it alone! In our changing world, many of us are separated from family and old friends. Make new contacts, stay active and get involved with new groups while maintaining your long distance relationships. Your enthusiasm, high self-esteem and positive energy will ripple throughout the entire family system.

In closing, I encourage you to cherish each of your children for his or her uniqueness. Express your appreciation often to them for the qualities that make them who they are. Self-esteem is the core ingredient for achieving success and happiness in all arenas of life. Building your child's self-esteem is a gift that your children will definitely treasure today, tomorrow and for many years to come.

Best Wishes,

Dr. Ingrid Schweiger

ABOUT THE AUTHOR

Dr. Ingrid Schweiger is known internationally for her work with families. The American Association of Marriage and Family Therapy recognized Dr. Schweiger for her innovative family education programs used in communities throughout the world. Dr. Schweiger has served on the faculties of the University of Massachusetts in Amherst, MA and The New School for Social Research in New York City. She co-authored *Teacher Stress and Burnout*, published by the National Education Association, and produced the award-winning documentary *Teen Suicide*. Dr. Schweiger's media experience includes hosting a live call-in radio show as well as frequent appearances on the NBC News in Massachusetts. She is a sought after speaker and seminar leader praised for her warm, dynamic style.

Dr. Schweiger maintains a private practice in New York City where she works with individuals, couples and families. In her free time, she enjoys spending time with her husband, children and adorable grandsons.

To learn more about seminars, teleconferences and coaching, visit:

www.Self-EsteemForALifetime.com

www.DrIngridSchweiger.com

Dr. Schweiger invites you to send your comments and questions to:

info@DrIngridSchweiger.com

Breinigsville, PA USA
11 October 2010
247116BV00001B/3/P